Making Clubs Work

A practical guide to creating
successful clubs, societies and other
membership organisations

BRAD PARKES

Making Clubs Work
A practical guide to creating successful clubs,
societies and other membership organisations
© Brad Parkes

paperback ISBN 978-1-909116-29-0
.epub ISBN 978-1-909116-30-6
.mobi ISBN 978-1-909116-31-3

Published in 2014 by SRA Books

The right of Brad Parkes to be identified as the author
of this work has been asserted by him in accordance with the
Copyright, Designs and Patents Act 1988.

A CIP record of this book is available from the British Library.

All rights reserved. No part of this book may be reproduced, stored
in a retrieval system, or transmitted in any form or by any means,
electronic, mechanical, photocopying, recording or otherwise,
without the prior written permission of the copyright holder.

No responsibility for loss occasioned to any person acting or
refraining from action as a result of any material in this publication
can be accepted by the author or publisher.

Dedication

From my past…
I'd like to dedicate this book to the memory of my dad. Thanks for
the hidden gems, the introductions to the world of clubs, and the
encouragement to be myself.

From my present…
I dedicate this book to all the members of all the clubs that I have had the
pleasure to work with, be associated with, and to have the privilege to call
friends, and those I do not know. I hope that through you and this book,
clubs will flourish and one by one we will make a difference to those
around us.

In my future…
I dedicate this book to my son, Luke, you bring me smiles and happiness
daily, and you have introduced me to the concept of unconditional love. I
hope that you and all your generation have clubs in abundance to benefit
from, I hope and trust you all learn to belong and live your lives in a
society of community spirit and belonging.

Lastly, I dedicate this work to those who have supported me through the
journey of bringing it to reality:

Mum – you've always been there – Love you x

My business partner and brother, Spence, who travelled the length
and breadth of the country with me and at all sorts of hours in the
development of the material contained within the book, and helping me
bring inspiration to others.

Lastly, to my best friend, my soul mate, my confidante, my coach, my
cheerleader, my encourager, my rock… thanks Tammy, for everything you
are, and everything we are. You are my everything. Love you loads x

Testimonials

'An interesting and insightful read.'
Cait Allen
Chief Executive, Round Table

'For me, Brad is truly world-class in the field of recruitment and retention of members in membership organisations, and this book sets out everything that anyone associated with any club at any level would need to know. This book is the gold standard that others will be compared to – its the mark of a champion.'
Leon Taylor
British Olympic silver medallist in diving, author and professional speaker

'This book is written in a style that makes it easy to read, and being centred on a main story made up of a number of anecdotes, stories and metaphors that allows the reader to explore their own reality and how the principles can be employed in their clubs or teams makes this a uniquely simple yet very effective volume.'
Dame Mary Perkins
Founder Specsavers Optical Group

'I'm not a great reader, but I was completely engaged by *Making Clubs Work*. Brad tackles the topic of leadership in a different way to anything else I have read on the subject. Through his personal and informal style he engages the reader, compelling them to read on, while provoking a lot of thought. I would classify this book as a great read, and recommend it to anyone with an interest in leadership in any organisation.'
Richard Hill
Player – Bath RFC, England and British Lions
Coach – Bath RFC, Worcester Warriors and Rouen

'Brad is a guy who "walks his talk", demonstrating his authority and understanding by simplifying a complex issue through this charming narrative.'
Angi Egan
Author and professional speaker

Acknowledgements

I would like to acknowledge and thank the following people for their contributions to this book in the modern TV talent show style... in no particular order:

Mr Vincent: thanks for the inspiration all those years ago, in that first O level maths class, for teaching us how to take the complex, and make it simple and in doing so make anything possible. Thanks for teaching me how to do sums! Thanks for allowing me to use your story as part of my story.

Richard: an amazingly passionate lecturer, inspirational boss, mentor and coach, and above all else a great friend. Thanks for being Alex, and allowing me to share your story as much as mine, and being such a large part of mine and Billy's story. You introduced me to Round Table and Spectacle Makers, and by doing so opened so many doors that have given me countless opportunities and experiences, the words thank you do not do justice to the debt of gratitude I owe you. Thanks literally for everything.

Angi: thanks for the belief, encouragement and support. For giving input at an early stage that was invaluable. Thanks too for introducing me to Sue and her team. Thanks for being a mate.

Ed: I have tried so hard to track you down, and I know you are out there somewhere, taking photos and sharing your expertise. Thanks for introducing me to Archie.

Lt Col John Salmon OBE, LLB: thank you for your input and guidance on all things 'Livery', within this book and outside of it.

Sakthival: thanks for your company in the UK and your hospitality in India. For the amazing work you have done and continue to do for Freedom Through Education well done, thank you and keep it up. Thank you too, of course, for providing the second part of the elephant story – words cannot do justice to what that experience meant.

Sarah, Sue and the SRA Team: thanks for helping me bring Archie to life, Sarah our weekly catch-ups and your writing guidance have been a source of laughter and insight, thanks for joining me on the journey. Sue, your unrelenting friendship and professional vision that gave me the platform to share my story in a professional and businesslike way, it's been a great year for me, and a tough one for you, so thanks for your determination and inspiration.

The Reviewers: thanks for being prepared to read the manuscript, and make comment, the testimonials are appreciated – thanks Leon, Cait, Richard and Dame Mary.

The Clubs: thanks to all the chairmen and members of clubs I have visited over the years, some of whom have been singled out as examples within the book. I hope if you recognise yourself as a 'negative' example, that you will appreciate no names or references will reveal who you are, and you will know that by having such examples we have together allowed others to find a better way, to improve and to maybe even survive.

The Members: thanks to all the members and leaders of all the clubs I've ever had the privilege to be a member of, a leader within, an associate of particularly, and not exclusively: Tenby Rugby Club (Dezzy), Greenhill Rugby (Hugh, Newman, JJ Williams & John Rees), Tenby Scouts (Tony and Mo), Tenby Brass Band (Eileen, Chris, Les & Ian), Duke of Edinburgh Awards, Lions, Association of British Dispensing Opticians, The Worshipful Company of Spectacle Makers (Gordon, Sue, Abi, Judith & Don), Specsavers, Speakers Academy (Andy, Gil, Don & Julie), Professional Speakers Association (David & Mike), WI, Ladies Circle, 41 Club, Tangent, and The Round Table Trust (Andrew, John, Mark, Dave & Stephen).

Round Table: the organisation that has played a huge part of my life for so long deserves a mention on its own, so that I can mention some of the friends who have offered support, encouragement, trust, inspiration, motivation, fellowship and friendship over the years. To the specific guys in Bourne End and Flackwell Heath, Edgbaston and Solihull, Heart of England Area 35 and the National Council and Board. There are members who had trust in my abilities: in the initial instance Gary – thanks mate;

the guys on the teams – in particular David, Norman and Nish, what a formidable team we were; the National Presidents I have had the pleasure and honour to work with – Richard, Graham, Peter, John K, Dave, John P, Jason, Stephen, and Steve.

Cheerleaders: there have been many but specifically to mention: David, Sharon, Vicky, Ruth, Stephen, Karen, Greg, Mel, Lee, Barry, Jim, Gil, Paul, Andy, Johnny, and Rich.

Characters: thanks to all of you who have lent me your name for one of the characters in the book. Coming up with names for the characters was one of the hardest things about writing the book for me, so if you see your name there whether a first or middle name, I hope you will recognise yourself, in the name, but not necessarily in the character. Thank you for featuring in there somewhere.

Archie: lastly, it would not be right to not mention Archie. Wherever you are today, I hope you run like you were still a puppy with ears flapping in the wind and chasing seagulls and forgetting to stop when you hit the sea. I hope you have not wagged your tail off, and that you have found love and comfort and think about me as much as I think about you. Thanks for listening to me rehearsing my material as we walked along tow paths, in fields and parks. Thanks for the name boy.

Contents

Foreword by Leon Taylor

Imagine, if you will, standing backwards balanced on your tip-toes. Imagine that you are 10m above water and on the edge of a diving platform. You are about to perform the exact same dive as your team mate, at the same time, and hit the water perfectly in unison. Add to that the atmosphere of an Olympic final, the largest crowd to date fall silent and you could hear a pin drop.

Get it right and that dive will define the rest of your career, maybe even your life. Get it wrong and all manner of possible injuries could also significantly, negatively define the rest of your life.

Speak to any athlete, any sports man or woman, speak to any leader in business or any successful person in their field, and they would tell you that while that moment defines you, the years of preparation that go into that moment and every preceding moment is what truly defines you. It is those preceding moments that create the opportunity that stands before you for you to grasp.

While diving is predominantly categorised as an 'individual' sport, we are all part of wider teams. At Olympic level this includes medics, physios, coaches, nutritionists, personal trainers, to name a few. At entry levels though most of us are members of a club, and we will form part of a team. Do you remember during the 2012 London Olympics when Tom Daly won his medal, and his team mates jumped into the pool to celebrate with him? It is an iconic image that illustrates that, even as individuals, we are part of a team or a club.

The success of a club requires a number of factors to be in place that create the environment where individuals can flourish and be the best that they can be. Those elements are illustrated beautifully in *Making Clubs Work*.

Subsequent to 2008 I retired from competitive diving, and have been privileged to fulfil other roles in other teams, whether that be as coach or mentor, presenting on television, or working with a team of other speakers at a conference or seminar.

I didn't realise until I sat down to analyse situations that the principles Brad covers are the very essence of what has been successful in the clubs I have enjoyed being a member of, and have been lacking in the clubs I did not enjoy being a part of.

Brad's work in unpicking the complexity of what makes a club work successfully, and what can sabotage a club, and then to painstakingly piece it back together, is masterful. He is obviously passionate about the subject, and his ability to convey what could be a complex conundrum in such a simple, fun, easy to understand way reflects Brad's personality and his ability to make it easy for the reader to get the message and implement it to achieve success.

Reading the stories and anecdotes in this book, I am sure, will have far further reaching impact than how to operate membership organisations. I am convinced that businesses, leaders, sports personalities and many others will be able to apply these principles into their everyday activities and not just limit to using them at their monthly or weekly meeting of their hobby organisation. That is what gives this book so much value to the reader – the principles have the ability to be used in lots of ways.

For me, Brad is truly world-class in the field of recruitment and retention of members in membership organisations, and this book sets out everything that anyone associated with any club at any level would need to know. This book is the gold standard that others will be compared to - its the mark of a champion.

Dive in and enjoy the read.

Introduction

Over a number of years, I have developed a passion for membership and membership organisations, and I believe our society and communities would be stronger and more pleasant places to live and work in if more people were members of more organisations.

As part of my work at Round Table, on the board and in membership teams, I have developed a structure around which a club can recruit and retain members. Recent years have seen me take that work, research and development and compile it into a book – this book.

The book is a collection of my own personal stories from my growing up years, and my observations and experiences in clubs and associations, with some helpful hints and tips of how to operate a successful club.

It is not my concern if an individual wishes to join one club or organisation or another. It does not matter if someone is a member of Round Table, Rotary, WI, Lions, Scouts, English Heritage, National Trust or a local reading club. What is important is that they get a sense of belonging, a pride in belonging, and a feeling of security by belonging.

What matters is that people belong.

Brad Parkes
May 2014

How this book can work for you

My aim in writing this book has been to make a difference – a difference to you as a member of a club or organisation, a difference to the club or organisation to which you belong, and a difference to the community at large.

What your needs are, and how you feel you can best support your club or organisation, will, of course, be distinctive and unique, and so I have tried to make this book as flexible as possible, in order for you to be able to read it in the way that works best for you, and take from it the information and advice that is most relevant to where you and your organisation are today.

The research that forms the basis of this book was originally carried out to provide the content and structure for a 36-hour training workshop, which I ran for guys in the club I was a member of at the time. This workshop provided a plan, a campaign, the inspiration and the motivation to save that club.

Later, I was asked to replicate this for the clubs in my area (there were about 12). It was felt that 36 hours was too much time, so I distilled it down to an 8-hour/one day workshop. This worked well and received awards, the greatest of which was the success of increasing the number of members across those clubs collectively by over 20% inside two years.

This success was later further recognised and I have since been asked to run workshops sharing these stories and the ideas across the UK, and internationally, at various meetings and conferences. The ideas and stories have been enhanced, added to, changed over time, and now have been distilled into a book that I hope everyone involved in the world of clubs and membership organisations will find useful.

The book is divided into three parts – a story, real-life examples and observations drawn from actual organisations, and a summary of key learning points. The story involves a young man called Billy, and his development into a thoughtful and helpful member of his community, through the guidance of a mentor called Alex. Billy's experiences are based on my own – either on things I went through myself, or else things I saw others go through. I have woven each one into an episode in Billy's development, and each episode in Billy's development also corresponds to a key area in terms of the successful development and growth of a membership organisation.

In this way, each crucial area of growth and development in a membership organisation is looked at from three different perspectives:

- through the story of Billy, Alex and a café called Archie's Place
- through examples and observations drawn from actual organisations
- through a series of key learning points

Whether you wish to read the book as a whole, moving through each chapter from story to examples to key learning points, or whether you simply would like to concentrate on the examples, or the key learning points, or just the stories, is entirely up to you and what suits you best. However you approach this book, I firmly believe there will be something here for you to learn and apply, to make your own club or organisation more focused, more popular, more successful.

There are also some pages at the back of the book left blank specifically to allow you to make notes on actions as they crop up in your mind, so that they are captured in the same place and contained between the same covers for future reference as you start putting your ideas into action.

Once you have read this book, I encourage you to log on to the website and register on the forum pages to share the ideas and thoughts that work for you www.makingclubswork.com. Here, you can also learn from those who are sharing their ideas and connect with others who are in the same boat or have been and have found a solution.

Enjoy the read!

Chapter One

Hidden Gems and Unlocked Doors

Chapter One Hidden Gems and Unlocked Doors

Billy started at the smell of not-quite burning but soon-to-be cinders toast. His mind had definitely been elsewhere. Lunging for the cooker, he whipped the toast out from under the grill and set it on a plate. Grabbing his coffee, he sat down at the table and tried to focus on simply eating his breakfast without starting a house fire. It was the morning of his very first appraisal.

He'd been working for BCH for just over a year now and he was excited and nervous in just about equal parts. Alex, his manager, was a great guy and Billy had already learned a lot from him. He really hoped he'd pleased Alex with the way he'd been working, but he knew he still had a long way to go. Strangely enough, he found himself really looking forward to the appraisal – it would be good to know how he was doing and what he could do better. More than anything, though, he was looking forward to spending the day with Alex – he just knew and understood so much, and Billy loved spending time with him.

Billy had first met Alex when the older man had done some part-time teaching at the college from which Billy graduated. Over his breakfast, Billy's mind wandered to the day he sat in a workshop conducted by Alex, remembering how he thought to himself, 'One day I'm going to work with him.'

Billy had been brought up in a family-run hotel in a seaside resort. The business had given him a fantastic foundation to working with teams and the public, as he had shared his house every week of the summer season with a new bunch of friends. He had learned from an early age that he had as big a part to play in the success of the business as anyone else in the team. His father would impress on him the importance of making friends and of making sure that those other kids had a great holiday: 'If the kids have a great holiday, they will be happy. Happy kids mean happy mums and dads. Happy mums and dads mean repeat business and recommendations.'

Billy had moved away from the seaside to the big city at the end of his schooling in order to go to college. He'd spent three years studying, had graduated and had then joined BCH at the beginning of the previous summer on their graduate scheme. Billy felt at ease at BCH – being part of a family-run business literally felt like a home from home to him.

Okay, it wasn't a hotel, but, Billy mused, the two businesses had a surprising amount in common. BCH was a family-run retail and manufacturing business. They designed, built and fitted kitchens and bathrooms and had been doing so for three generations, having gained a reputation for service and reliability together with consistently fair pricing and high-quality workmanship. The company had expanded over the years, growing from three small, local showrooms to now operating out of 100 showrooms across the country, together with a large manufacturing plant, warehouse and distribution under the 'group' umbrella. They had even recently acquired sites that extracted and supplied all the raw materials they used.

*****

Alex, Billy's manager, had been with the firm about 15 years. Like Billy, he'd joined BCH on their graduate scheme and he'd stayed with the company ever since. He thought it likely that he'd stay with the company until he retired. Not through a lack of ambition, and certainly not because they paid exceptionally well, but more because, now that he had joined the board, he clearly saw just how well the company's values and his were aligned.

During his years at BCH, Alex had discovered he was a great salesman – not because he bullied prospects or had a 'system' for 'closing the sale', but simply because he really enjoyed discovering the customer's vision and understanding what the finished job would be like for them. He always put the customer's needs ahead of his own, and supplied what was right for them and not what was right for him or the business. Other graduates had come and gone over the years, most making a name for themselves with increased one-off sales, but Alex had outperformed them all with repeat business and the trust of his clients. If he'd wanted, he could have had the shortest buying cycle of all sales team members.

Alex had been the fastest graduate to be promoted to manager and had been given the responsibility to train up all new graduates joining the organisation. The company recognised that Alex was skilled at guiding new recruits through their early months, demonstrating to them how to uphold the company's values and how to engage with the business while putting the customer at the centre of all that they do. Despite these added responsibilities, Alex maintained a regular sales role and the responsibility for overseeing 12 units in a region – the largest region in the group. Alex instilled in all the unit employees under his guidance a happy, friendly demeanour and, as a result, they consistently outperformed other stores and regions.

Whereas other managers held on to their knowledge or contained individuals' potential in fear that they might threaten them in their role, Alex identified that if he encouraged progression and continued to support and develop his team, they would all grow, all get better and all achieve more. As subordinates grew into their next job, they did not depose Alex, but they allowed him to grow and develop into his next job too. Alex also held the best staff retention figures in the whole of the business.

Alex made a commitment to all his graduate trainees to share all his knowledge and expertise with them so that they too might use that knowledge to be the best leaders they could be. He shared his unique proven steps to success with them all, and encouraged them to put this shared knowledge and learning into practice so that they could be the best they could be. He knew that his reputation was reflected in what they did, not in what he did alone.

*****

Billy was sitting at his breakfast table, considering what the day ahead and his appraisal held in store for him. He felt he had worked hard during the year. He had achieved some great results and he had always wanted to do his best for himself and for Alex.

In his mind, Billy was taken back to the moment when he realised that all the students on his course were applying for their first jobs. Billy had already secured his. He still had his father's words ringing in his ears. The words hadn't meant that much at the time but now, in hindsight, looking back on what the future had bestowed on him since then, they brought a smile to his face.

Sometimes, Billy realised later, we don't appreciate the full significance or meaning of messages we are given at the time. The key to unlocking our potential is to understand this and to remain open to all the advice we receive, remembering the messages so that when the time is right we can act upon them. In his own mind, Billy referred to these messages as 'hidden gems'.

Billy's father had been a heavy smoker – an addiction that would eventually take his life. When Billy was little, they would all travel as a family to the city to shop, especially at Christmas time. Billy would stick with his dad, and would often accompany his father outside shops as he smoked a cigarette while his mother would be inside shopping.

One day, a particularly busy Christmas shopping day, Billy recalled the shops having been full of people. There had been a sense of hustle and bustle on the streets, the smell of roasting chestnuts, pine and Christmas had filled the air. There had been a real buzz with busy people chatting and wishing each other season's greetings. Shops and streets had been festooned with trees, lights, decorations and artificial snow. The atmosphere had been electric. Billy had loved it.

He and his dad had been standing outside one particular large department store, one they often stood outside. The main entrance was made up of 12 doors.

'See that, son,' his dad had said to Billy. 'See how the majority of people fight to get through the open door while others make a quicker entry by pushing on the closed door.'

Billy had watched for a moment to observe exactly what his father had pointed out. Some of the doors had been open, held open by customers passing through them, holding them for the people following behind, each person holding the door for a few seconds only and the door being almost suspended in a permanent open position as if broken or held on a latch.

There were other doors that had been closed. They had been unlocked, but they had remained closed. Billy had watched as one member of the public approached and chose to push on one of the unlocked closed doors. As they had passed through it, a line of people had followed them and the door had remained open. The flow of people through one of the other doors had slowed until eventually the door had closed and remained so for quite some time.

Billy had decided to test the theory. He had deliberately gone over to open a closed door to observe how people would change direction, almost falling over themselves, to gain access through the newly-opened door. He had then moved to another door that had been closed and opened that one instead. This test had amused Billy during quite a number of 'cigarette breaks' over the years.

Billy had also remembered his father's words when he had begun applying for work. He realised that the jobs advertised on notice boards and in magazines were the jobs everyone else was applying for. The open door factor was in operation again. Therefore, Billy had taken it upon himself to research a list of companies he'd like to work for that were not advertising jobs. He had prioritised them and then written to them enquiring if they had considered taking on a newly-qualified graduate. He had reasoned that it was better to be one of a handful of candidates applying for the jobs not being advertised rather than one in a hundred applying for the jobs that were.

Top of Billy's list had been Alex's company, but the list had had about 15 other names on it. Billy had been invited to eight interviews from those letters; the other seven companies had all sent nice letters declining the application. Of the eight interviews, Billy had secured five job offers.

The day Billy had received the letter from BCH offering him employment with them under Alex's leadership was a day Billy would always remember. The offer had not been the best financially, it was not the closest to home and it was neither the latest nor the most modern of places to work, but the decision had been easy. He had accepted BCH's offer and had written letters to the other four organisations explaining his reasons for declining – he had been conscious that he might need to contact them again one day.

Billy was to uncover many more hidden gems before his time with BCH was over.

*****

The appraisal went well. Alex had a great way about him, being able to make feedback constructive rather than negative, and praise good work in a sincere manner that left Billy feeling motivated, inspired and with his self-esteem stronger than previously.

During the appraisal, Alex highlighted Billy's strengths and weaknesses and, between them, they began to formulate a personal development plan.

'So, what's your dream then, Billy?' asked Alex.

'I want to be a great leader like you!' Billy exclaimed, then blushed as he caught himself embarrassingly idolising his boss.

'That's good,' responded Alex, with a warm generous smile on his face that melted Billy's embarrassment. 'And when you are a great leader, Billy, who or what do you want to be leading?'

'I want to be a manager, or even have my own firm one day.'

'That's a great vision, Billy. You know, I reckon one day you will.'

They set out a programme that would teach Billy everything he would need to know to become a great leader. Whether it was the leader of a shop, a team or a business, Alex knew he would impart everything Billy would need.

Alex had devised a fabulous programme and had taken a number of his graduates through the process over the years. Alex had enlisted the help of colleagues and acquaintances whom he had met through a club who would each teach Billy what he needed to know. Alex would introduce Billy to them all in time. Alex had identified that what his club had learned about recruiting and retaining members would reveal the skills and principles that would help any willing graduate become an outstanding leader. Alex did not share the details of the programme with Billy. He had learned it was best to reveal the stages one at a time, when his junior was ready.

Alex was always amazed how much the skills people learned from being a member of a club, society or organisation could benefit the workplace, and vice versa. If more people realised this, then maybe more would get more involved. Alex's wish was that one day many more people would get involved in their community, be it at work or during their leisure time, contribute to their environment and, in doing so, make the world a better place for everyone. He had learned over the years that the principles he would share with Billy would be as useful and relevant to football, golf, squash, rugby or any other sports clubs as they would be to any service club, church congregation, as well as any workplace. The leadership skills apply to all leaders, whether they are a club chair, captain of a team, team leader in the workplace or elder in a church. The list and application is endless. Alex hoped one day, through many of his students, to impact the wider communities.

'And to help you get there you need to understand the principles of "backward planning"...,' Alex continued.

Alex was one of those successful managers who was able to get the best out of those who worked with him. Everyone who worked with him trusted him. He gave them opportunities and they repaid him with loyalty. Alex took pride in seeing those working with him grow, flourish and sometimes move on to pastures new, like fledglings flying the nest when the time was right. He knew his success would be measured by the success of those he had mentored.

'Will you tell me about "backward planning" please?' asked an excited Billy.

'Of course, let's get together again next week.'

Over the years, I have had the pleasure of working with some amazingly talented and dedicated people. None more so than in the sports arena where most of us know the time, effort and dedication that has to go into being successful.

I have been pleased to have worked for a number of years with several football managers in top-flight roles. Working with, on the whole, a great bunch of guys who are dedicated and committed to their sport, and in many cases fighting the rigours and fickleness of modern-day sporting leadership. On those days, I am so pleased I am not 'into' football and never have been, as it would otherwise be easy to become star struck. Frankly, it's sometimes best I don't know the names before I meet the guys.

I am reminded of one particularly nice guy who had been manager at a club in the second or third level of the English game and had recently been made redundant. We met while he was looking for work. We talked and I shared Dad's principle of pushing on unlocked doors.

About six months later, I got an SMS text message saying, 'This is my new number.' That exchange resulted in him sharing with me that he had 'pushed on some unlocked doors' and landed himself a job in a more significant role and club than ever before.

KEY LEARNINGS

Pushing on an open door: this is a very interesting concept and one that is often hard for people who are not looking for work to get their head around. It is also sometimes hard for folk to see how this can apply to a club or a society. It works in two ways.

Firstly, we need to consider our club as one of those doors. If we want to attract the largest number of people through our door, we need to demonstrate that our door is open. We need to find the ways that allow the people who would walk through an open door to walk through our door, and ensure that those who would avoid the unlocked closed door do not perceive our door to be locked and so closed to them. The fear of rejection will often mean most of the population will not approach a door and try it to see if it is open or not.

This makes a clear distinction from those clubs or groups who thrive on exclusivity and prefer there to be a perception that they are only open to a select band. And, in many cases, this works for them nicely.

Secondly, we need to consider that there are groups of prospective members in our communities. There are members of the public who want to be a member of an organisation, they want to belong. Some may even be looking for exactly what we offer, but don't know we exist. We need to push on the doors that get us to these groups of people. We should also be mindful that if we don't, another organisation may well do soon.

Chapter Two

Crossing Streams and Backward Planning

Chapter Two Crossing Streams and Backward Planning

It was a balmy summer's evening. The sun was still high in the sky, the air warm and the hint of backyard barbecues drifted through the streets. People wandered at ease across the town's central square, half dazed by the unaccustomed heat of the day. Some sat on the stone border to the central fountain, enjoying the cool air given off by the tumbling water. Around the square stood tall, old houses, long since converted to apartments on the upper floors, while the ground floors now consisted of a mixture of restaurants, cafés, shops, a tourist centre and a few offices housing lawyers, accountants and other similar professions.

The cafés and restaurants had seating set up outside – a mixture of wooden and metal weather-resistant tables and chairs. A number of them sported large parasols and outdoor heaters, so that no matter what the weather patrons could sit outside and watch the world go by. Each restaurant and café had its own distinctive colour scheme, so that even from across the square each outlet could be distinguished. The square was an array of colour and looked bright, fun and sophisticated.

On this particular evening, the parasols were collapsed to allow the last of the evening sun to cascade on to the glowing faces of local people enjoying some rest on their way home from work, their features adorned with a fabulous display of sunglasses.

Alex and Billy were sitting at a table outside a café on the south side of the plaza under the distinctive blue parasols of Alex's favourite café. They ordered coffee and made small talk as the world went about its business.

Alex respected those who went further than simply keeping their heads down and doing their jobs. He liked it when his team members appreciated his time and experience and put themselves out knowing there would be a greater reward to come. Those who would join him for a coffee in the square, attend a meeting 'out of hours' or do something extra for the firm without demanding overtime knew that the wisdom, experience or security they would receive was priceless.

Over the years, Alex had seen a number of graduates come and go. Some came and left stronger, others left weaker than when they had arrived. Those who had developed most, those who went on to greater things, those who went on to achieve their dreams, were those who put themselves out.

'You only get out what you put in,' explained Alex. 'To get to be the best is not easy. Staying there is even harder.'

Billy was visibly excited about having another meeting with Alex and could barely keep still in his seat. His head was spinning with the concept of 'backward planning' – what it could mean, how he would use it, how it would help him achieve his goals, how it would bring him success and what was 'backward planning' anyway?

'Will you share your secrets about "backward planning" with me?' asked Billy, with a mixture of impatience and enthusiasm.

'No,' said Alex. 'I can't.'

'Oh,' said Billy. His face fell.

'Not because I don't want to, Billy, but because you must learn these things for yourself.'

'Well, how can I learn them if I don't know what they are?'

Alex left the question unanswered. 'Come with me,' he said, getting up from the table. Billy pushed his chair back and got up, puzzled as to what was going on. Alex left payment and, together, Billy and Alex walked across the square.

Not much was spoken between the two men on their short walk. Billy was still pondering the questions in his head, while Alex strode on with a confident and self-assured step.

On the outskirts of the town, Alex and Billy came to a quaint, old, stone bridge over a wide stream, not quite wide enough to be considered a river. They stopped on the bridge and looked over at the flowing water below.

'Perfect,' said Alex, as he turned on his heels to retrace his steps from the middle of the bridge towards town.

Billy was utterly bemused, but followed curiously behind.

Where the bridge wall ended there was an old, metal kissing gate, through which they passed on to steps that led down to the bank alongside the stream that ran under the bridge. They walked along the towpath for a short distance and then came to a halt alongside a large, stone boulder that had been turned into a seat. Alex settled himself on the boulder.

'No,' Alex said firmly, as Billy started to join him. 'Not you. Not yet anyway. First, you'll need to take off your shoes and socks and roll your trouser legs up.'

'Why?'

'So you can learn about "backward planning". Unless, of course, you've forgotten, or want to change your mind?'

'Yes, of course. I mean, no, I mean…' Billy stopped talking and slipped his shoes off, removed his socks and rolled his trousers up as instructed. He stood before Alex feeling vulnerable and silly.

'Okay, off you go then… cross the stream.'

'What?'

'Cross the stream. There are plenty of stepping stones scattered around. Use them to cross the stream without getting your feet wet. The explanation for "backward planning" is on the other side.'

Excited at the prospect of finding out about 'backward planning', Billy set off. He identified the first largest boulder and stepped across to it, then looked around to spot a second, then a third and a fourth.

Billy was about half way across the stream and was feeling quite good about himself when he realised there were no more stepping stones. The opposite bank was far out of reach. He looked around and, after a few moments, saw more stones to his right. He stepped back to the stone he was previously standing on and from here he could step across to another stone, and yet another. He managed to get to a point that was further across than when he'd turned back before, but not much further.

He retraced his steps again and found another series of stones that took him to about three-quarters of the way across before once again he reached a dead end.

After retracing his steps a number of times and after about half an hour of standing on tiptoes on hard rocks coated with cold water, Billy's heart was sinking. He went back to the bank and found another stone from which to start his journey.

The same sequence of trial and error carried on for a further half an hour until, eventually, he reached the other bank. With cold feet and a hot and sweaty forehead, and with excitement but little energy to express it, he looked around for his answer.

'I don't see anything over here, Alex,' he called.

Alex had been sitting reading a book for the hour while Billy worked his way across the stream. He looked up from his book, waved and gestured by cupping his ear that he didn't hear Billy.

'I said,' Billy shouted, with his hands cupping his mouth making an impromptu loudhailer, 'I don't see anything over here!'

'What do you mean?' Alex called back.

'You said the explanation for "backward planning" was on this side of the stream.'

'No I didn't.'

'Yes you did.'

'No. What I actually said was the explanation for "backward planning" was on the other side. Where is the other side to you now?' He didn't allow enough time for the answer. 'You had better come on back.'

Billy was feeling quite dejected, thinking Alex had deliberately humiliated him. These feelings turned to anger as he bounded his way back across the stream, retracing his successful route.

'Why did you do that?'

'Do what?' asked Alex.

'Why did you make me go all the way over there, getting cold, wet, tired and frustrated, when the explanation was here all the time?'

'Sometimes, Billy, what we want is here all along, but we have to go there and back to appreciate it.' Alex said, ignoring Billy's outburst and questions. 'How long did it just take you to cross the stream the second time, Billy?'

'I don't know.'

'Just under seven minutes,' declared Alex. 'That's quite a good effort. How long did it take you to get across it from this side to that?'

'Ages.'

'Sixty two minutes,' Alex said, checking a scribbling on the inside front cover of his book.

'So?'

'So, Billy, how were you able to cross the stream so quickly the second time?'

'Well, I already knew the route I was going to take.'

'And, from the other bank, how many stones were there from which you could start your return journey?'

'Erm,' Billy glanced back over his shoulder to check. 'I'm not sure, but just the one I think. Why?'

'That's right. There is only one stone you can reach from the other bank or, more importantly, when looking from this side, there is only one stone from which you can reach the far bank.'

Billy was still puzzled, but now intrigued as to where this was going.

'When you were working out your way to cross the first time, you set off with blind ambition following the route so many have before you.

That route serves only to teach us that trial and error expends lots of energy, time and effort. However, if you had taken a moment to plan your journey backwards, you would have seen that the only stone to allow you to reach the far bank was that one,' Alex pointed in the direction of the furthest stone. 'With that information you could ask yourself – which stone do I need to get to that will enable me to step across to the last stone? – and the answer would have been that one,' and Alex pointed towards the next stone in Billy's return route.

'And then I'd have seen that to get to there, I'd have to reach there, there and there,' said Billy, reinvigorated that he was now beginning to understand, pointing at all the stones he had used to make his second crossing in sequence.

'That's right, Billy. Have you ever heard of the old wife's saying: "A stitch in time"'?'

'Saves nine?'

'Yes, and had you thought about your route beforehand and planned your route backwards, you'd have crossed first time as you did the second time in seven minutes and not taken nine times as long. That is the principle of "backward planning", Billy. You see why I thought it important for you to learn – and to learn through experience?'

Billy nodded. 'Can we meet next week so I can buy you a coffee this time, please?'

'Sure, sounds good to me. Same time, same place.'

I have been involved in and worked with a number of organisations over the years. One, in particular, springs to mind as a wonderful example of the power of investment into a long-term strategy.

The organisation in question used to exhibit the classic symptoms of a lack of a cohesive, club agreed and adopted long-term plan. I call this 'one-year-ism'. This led to the organisation lurching in one direction under one leader one year, only to head off in another direction under a different leader the next.

All leaders were very positively motivated, had good intentions and acted in the best interests of the organisation, yet 'one-year-ism' drove the organisation to be stagnant when it was required to take concerted and consistent action. (The 'rubber ring principle' in chapter 8 (page 93) illustrates this.) The debilitating actions were apparent at a number of levels within the organisation – at local club level, at county level and at national governing body level too.

This cycle was broken with very dynamic effect. The organisation underwent a refocus on what was important and the results that needed to be achieved. A restructure then followed in line with achieving those goals, which included reversing declining membership into growth and a change to how the organisation would be governed and run. A long-term plan and strategy was set out, agreed and implemented under the watchful eye of an appointed long-term leader, not an elected short-term leader.

Research shows that successful clubs and organisations have an employed or appointed leader in the guise of a chief executive officer, or other such title. In most of these successful organisations, this role is also conducted by someone from 'outside' the organisation – at least in the original instance – which allows them to remain removed from the 'internal politics' and focus on the strategic matters at hand.

The plan needs to set out objectives and activities that will remain no matter who is elected as the figurehead of the organisation. They also need to be regularly reviewed, updated and reset. In essence, the whole organisation needs to agree to adopt this structure so that all future elected officers of the organisation follow the same path – knowing they are being elected to deliver that plan, not to recreate their own plan.

A very descriptive metaphor has been shared with me – it's like a train travelling on a journey from A to B. The train will stop at various stations along the way. At those stations, some passengers will get off and new ones will embark. The train, however, will continue along the same track to the same original destination. The passengers who embark get on to the train knowing the destination and the route, and they may well leave the train at a subsequent station along that journey.

In a relatively very short period of time, the decline in membership numbers slowed, stopped and reversed.

In a club of which I was a member, we implemented a plan over a longer term, breaking the annual cycle. Three chairs were elected in one meeting and a three-year plan was agreed upon. The policies and procedures were reviewed and modified to reflect how the club needed to operate. This all resulted is successful membership growth. I understand that many companies in the Far East nowadays work on business plans in excess of a hundred years.

How long did it take to create the pyramids in Egypt or the Great Wall of China?

For great projects, what is absolutely clear is that the leaders have to understand that they may not see the project through to its end. Most great clubs will be in existence far beyond the current membership and, therefore, the plan and route should not reflect today's people but what future members want in order to attract them in the first place and provide the plan for the route they will follow – while allowing some 'tweaks' only on 'how' the plan is implemented.

In order to create a master plan, one must first see things exactly as they are. Hold up the mirror and take a good, long, hard look at what is seen. See it for exactly what it is – the truth.

Once we know exactly what we have and where we stand, only then can we begin to dream about where we'd like to be. That image of what we want to achieve must not only be clear, it also has to be compelling. It must be compelling not only to the current membership, but also to the future membership whom we don't yet even know. It is only once the assessment is complete and the vision is created that we can begin to create the reality. It is a reality that will be adopted and enhanced by future generations, and it is a reality that the current members have to accept is not 'theirs' but the 'club's'.

My late ex-father-in-law was an avid gardener and he would often say – the work you do today is not for today or tomorrow, but for next year and the years beyond that.

Members of clubs would always do well to realise that the work they do today will only bear fruit for a future generation of members, which they have an obligation and responsibility to fulfil today.

KEY LEARNINGS

Is your club or organisation as successful as you'd like it to be? What changes do you need to make, and how will they affect your members?

'Change' is not a word that many people like to hear, especially those who are 'belongers' in the world. There are many psychological profiling studies that have concluded that 'belongers' like things to stay as they are. They like tradition and they certainly do not like change.

Change does not have to mean turning circles into squares, though it can mean turning circles into spheres.

Any plan is only as good as the whole club's ability to implement the plan and, therefore, everyone must be on board. To do this, there must be an understanding that by acceptance we do not mean agreement. What I mean here is that most clubs, societies and teams get bogged down in the detail and in trying to reach consensus and, yet, in business there is always a single leader who – given an impasse – will call time on the discussion and make a decision.

If teams can agree from the outset that the process may involve them in accepting a way forward even if not everyone agrees with it, then the team is more likely to succeed. There has to be a similar acceptance that if it is not 'my idea' it's not necessarily wrong – we have to be open to others' valued input and we must, therefore, give them a voice. There are times in some clubs where it is those who shout the loudest who get heard. Great leaders are able to give quiet voices air time so they can be heard in equal measure. They will be the leaders who succeed.

Map out where it is you want to go, then how you will get there. Check out the stepping stones along the way and be as clear on the path as you can be before you choose to set off.

Chapter Three

Two Ears and
Four Stones

Chapter Three Two Ears and Four Stones

'There you are sir,' said the waiter, as he placed a coffee on the table in front of Alex, 'And you too, young sir.'

The waiter was wearing his usual pristine uniform. Shoes polished so you could see your face in them, black trousers with crisp creases, a white cotton shirt that was neatly ironed and finished with a black tie. His black tie, however, was not tucked inside his shirt like most other waiters, it was held in place by a tie clip, attached low down on the tie so it stopped the tail dangling anywhere it shouldn't. The tie clip was worn not just for ornamental reasons but for practical ones. Around his waist, the waiter had an apron that was spotless, starched and embroidered across one corner elegantly with the name of the establishment – Archie's Place.

Billy couldn't wait to start telling Alex what a great week he'd had. Not only had his sales figures been the highest yet, but he had also been working hard at 'backward planning' his future. He set out all his plans and dreams with Alex sitting, listening intently, not judging, not dampening his enthusiasm, just listening.

Listening was a skill Alex had acquired years before from his mentor Bob. Bob's favourite saying was, 'God gave you two of these,' pointing to his ears, 'and one of these,' pointing to his mouth, 'and we should use them in those proportions.' Bob had taught Alex to listen to himself and to others intently and to ask questions that sought to clarify the meaning of what was being said. This had made Alex outstanding in his field, not only within the firm but within the industry, being invited to become a visiting lecturer and examiner of undergraduates in the fields of management and business, as well as in his own field of artistic design and technical drawing. It was that recognition that had led Alex to lecture at Billy's college and that, ultimately, led to their original meeting.

While Alex listened, nodded, smiled, encouraged and gave his colleague the time and space, Billy painted the biggest, brightest picture of his future. Alex only intervened to ask him to paint greater detail and splash greater colour on the canvas of his dreams. Once he had painted all the intricate detail, Billy then began to tell Alex how his experience the week before had allowed him to start to identify the stepping stones he needed to reach to enable him to reach his goal.

'This is fabulous work,' encouraged Alex.

Alex had seen similar enthusiasm and energy in those who went on to great success, and he mirrored Billy's enthusiasm. Billy felt he was the first who had ever set out such grand ideas.

Eventually, when Billy had run out of steam, Alex proffered, 'I think it is time I introduced you to some friends of mine. They will be able to help you obtain the skills you need to turn your dreams into reality.'

'That sounds interesting. Who are they?'

'I am part of a group of mates who get together regularly to do all sorts of activities that help us to grow as we play, develop when we least expect it and to try out new challenges in a safe place with friends around you.'

'What sort of activities?'

'Just about everything you've ever wanted to do, and all the things everyone else wants to do, so you get to do things you never even thought of enjoying and sometimes things you never even thought were possible.'

'That sounds fun, but how will that help me?' asked Billy, inquisitively.

'Just imagine for a moment that your dream that you painted so beautifully earlier is a house, your home say. You would want it built on strong foundations wouldn't you?' Alex didn't wait for an answer to the rhetorical question, and continued, 'Well, this group will help you to identify the four strong foundation stones upon which great leaders are built. Then, by watching, listening and doing, you too will become a great leader, whether it is in a firm, on your own or part of a club. You will stand on the strong foundations of great leaders.'

'So, what are the four foundation stones of leadership?'

'Remember crossing the stream?'

'Yes.' Billy was transported to his earlier learning during which he realised that he needed to temper his headless chicken approach and take a more considered one.

'The four foundation stones of leadership are: greatness, identify opportunities, *carpe diem* and nurture. However, before you can learn about these you must first learn about the seven dream stealers that lie in wait.'

'The dream stealers?' quizzed Billy.

'Yes,' Alex went on. 'The things that stand in your way of success, the things that can, and do, bring down what might otherwise be great organisations, teams, firms or clubs.'

'Where can I learn about the dream stealers?'

Alex scribbled two telephone numbers with names alongside them on the back of his business card. 'Here, take this and call John.'

Billy looked down and read the name 'John' alongside one of the numbers. He read the number back to Alex. Alex did not have the most legible handwriting in the world, and he smiled to himself knowing Billy had learned already to clarify information to ensure he had the information correctly understood.

'Tell him I told you to call him – that you've heard about how great the club is that he is a member of and you are interested to learn more. The second number is for Pete, but only call him if you really need to, okay?'

Billy read out the number and added, 'But only call Pete if I really need to.'

Being clear about your outcomes, your goals and your intent is critical in so many ways.

Firstly, if you do not know precisely what it is you want to create, how will you know which direction to head in? Think about it. When you are planning a journey by car, you will first obtain your destination before consulting a map to plot out the possible routes. Once you have the options, you can choose the route that is best, and you will also know enough that if something diverts you along the way you can get back on track quickly and resume your journey.

Secondly, if you don't know what your destination is, there is a risk you will sail straight past it when you get there. This can mean you can arrive and not know it, you may not know how close you are at any point in time and you will not know when to celebrate the success of arriving. The middle point here is important, because many people, firms and clubs give up just before achieving success.

While climbing Mount Kinabalu, in Borneo, a group of climbers broke their hike down into small manageable chunks to focus on one small part of the mountain at a time. The trail is sectioned and flagged by marker posts every half a kilometre of the 8.5km trek. At each marker post the team celebrated, they shared high fives, stopped to drink, chat and laugh. The team spent the night in the final base camp called Laban Rata, which is nestled into the hills, amongst the cloud at an altitude of 3272m with 2km of trail to the summit remaining.

The next morning, the team set off for the summit to see the sun rise and then descend the mountain. One team member stopped, feeling sick and unable to complete the trek. To save hindering the others, they suggested that the rest of the team pushed on to make the summit. Later, when the group reassembled, it became apparent that the individual who had stopped had literally stopped 50m from the 7.5km (1km to go) marker. Had they known and seen that marker, the belief in their ability to continue to reach the summit may have been all they needed to reach the top.

I have seen many clubs suffer from a lack of vision, and a lack of vision that might deliver the results they deserve. I recall working with one organisation that wanted to increase its membership numbers. The organisation had a dozen leaders on its Board, the majority of whom saw their vision being to manage declining membership, off-load assets and close the shutters. There was one member of that Board who had the vision, the drive, the passion and the desire not to let the organisation fold. The ideas of that individual were eventually shared by others and the organisation is now achieving success in terms of membership growth.

There are professional bodies, governing bodies and industry societies that have suffered despite members having no choice but to be members, who have seen increases in membership when they listen to their members and prospective members and then deliver what the members are asking for – whether it be indemnity insurance at bulk purchased prices, legal advice, continued or higher education, development or training programmes, or a body which the members can be engaged with, proud of, and supported by.

What is absolutely imperative from the outset of any programme or campaign is to ensure every member has a part to play and plays their part to support the greater good.

The critical rule to have adopted is one of 'acceptance over agreement'. By definition, many membership organisations are run by consensus and, as such, most struggling groups suffer from being unable to agree on anything let alone a way forward. What is crucial is that all members agree that acceptance is good enough to get moving. We do not all have to agree on a way forward, but we do all have to accept the majority decision on what is the direction we will move in. Agreeing to accept before any discussions begin will help in the event of any subsequent dispute.

It is also key to ensure that all members are given the opportunity to contribute, no matter what their age, experience, background or how long they have been a member. All views are important. It is also very important to seek the views of non-members and to ask them why they are not a member. This can give amazing insight into what the final 'product' or 'offering' should be in order to attract the desired members.

Once we are clear on where we want to go and how we are going to get there, then we can begin to work on moving forward.

It is very powerful to listen to the views of others, ask pertinent questions and ask questions that elicit the information you require. Make sure, too, that you allow people the space, time and respect to answer questions fully, honestly and without any fear of recriminations. This can be particularly difficult as feedback is often taken as personal criticism or challenge. We have to avoid thinking in these terms and accept the feedback as it is – an insight of another's view of our world. This can be done in a number of ways: a one-to-one discussion or telephone conversation; a paper questionnaire or survey; or, very cheaply, quickly and easily, by an online survey provider.

This business is known as 'market research' – researching *who* is your key market and *what* it is they are looking for. If what they are asking for is not something you are offering, then you have to make the following decisions:

- Do we want to change what we provide?
- Do we want to change who we look to attract?
- Will we close if we do not change?
- What are our foundation stones?
- What is the small number of things upon which we hang our hat?
- What are our values?

Getting clarity and acceptance of our foundation stones, no matter what the number, will help us to understand and gain clarity on who our core market is and, therefore, how to attract it.

Chapter Four

Goldilocks and the Two Pubs

Chapter Four Goldilocks and the Two Pubs

'Your coffees, sirs.'

'Thanks, Archie,' said Billy to the waiter. He liked being called 'sir' and, despite telling the waiter he could call him Billy, he never did. He liked Archie all the more for that.

'So, how did you get on with John, and at his club?' asked Alex.

Billy visibly squirmed in his seat as the question made him uncomfortable. He had been asked to attend a meeting by his mentor, with people he knew to be his friends, and had not had the experience he had expected. He didn't want to offend the guru by telling him what an awful time he had had.

'Okay,' said Billy, quite coyly.

Alex was an expert in reading body language which obviously gave Billy's real thoughts away. These thoughts were the thoughts Alex had expected, and this was precisely the purpose of the exercise. He was pleased that Billy was about to uncover a number of hidden gems. He was also pleased that Billy's response was respectful and courteous towards Alex and his 'friends' – who were really more acquaintances than friends.

'And the truth sounds like...?' asked Alex.

'Really, it was okay.'

'Only okay?'

'Yes, I suppose so.'

'It seems you have learned diplomacy skills already, Billy,' continued Alex. 'That is a great skill to have. There are so many people out there who alienate themselves by expressing their opinions too quickly, opening their mouths without engaging their brains. However, as a great leader, you have to be able to see things as they are. Neither better nor worse. It's the Goldilocks factor.'

'The Goldilocks factor?'

'Yes, not too far one way, not too far the other. It's just right as it really is.'

The two laughed at Alex's analogy. Then, after a short amount of further small talk, Alex got them back on track.

'So, how was the club?'

'Well, it wasn't quite what I was expecting,' admitted Billy.

'In what way?'

'Well, I thought I was going there to learn about the four key elements of dynamic leadership.'

'So, what did you experience then?' encouraged Alex.

'Well, you asked me to call John. I did. There was no answer, so I left a message. Two days later, I called him again and his wife answered. She was very pleasant and she said she'd pass on my number and ask him to call me. He never did. After a week or so, I didn't know what else to do and remembered that you gave me a second number, for Pete.'

'And you should only...'

'...call him if I needed to,' Billy finished Alex's sentence. 'He seemed really annoyed that I had called him. Like I was interrupting him, like I was a distraction to him. He did, however, tell me when and where the club was meeting.'

'So how did that make you feel?' prompted Alex.

'Well, I nearly didn't bother going, to be honest. It seemed to me like they didn't really want me there, couldn't be bothered and certainly it was not a warm welcome.'

'But you did go, right?' asked Alex anxiously, as he wanted his protégé to get the whole learning experience.

'Yes, but I really was not comfortable. I nearly gave up. Then I remembered what you had said by the stream, that what we are looking for is sometimes there all along. I remembered learning by getting it wrong, even though it felt humiliating at the time.'

'The way you learn to ride a bicycle is to fall off occasionally and sometimes that hurts,' pointed out Alex.

Billy went on to explain his experiences of the meeting he went along to.

*****

The club had met at an old traditional pub. It seemed like a 'local drinkers' pub, the kind that you could imagine in a Western movie where everyone stops talking and looks at you as you walk through the door. The lighting was dim, the decor was tired, the lamp shades dusty, the pattern on the carpet had almost disappeared under stains and the air was filled with a mixture of stale beer and cooking fat. There was a jukebox, a fruit machine and a game machine, which all looked like they'd seen better days, and appeared to have not been used since those better days. The place looked like it had been neglected by the landlord over the years.

Part of the pub was sectioned off to create a seating area with tables and chairs that the pub promoted loosely as a restaurant. Billy turned up at the venue and bought himself a drink at the bar. He looked around the bar and saw a bunch of guys at one end laughing, joking and dressed casually with an array of modern, business, fashionable shirts, some of which Billy couldn't help admiring. He observed as another man entered the venue, approached them and asked if they were the group he was due to meet with. They welcomed him warmly, introduced him to all the men there and, while he was being introduced, a drink was being bought for him by another member of the group. He watched as they continued their conversation and one member of the group took a caring approach, explaining to the guest what they were talking about.

At the other end of the bar another group of men stood. There was not the same level of energy. They were dressed more conservatively, more traditionally, in suits and ties, or with blazers and ties. Some of the men had medals hanging from their chest pocket and some had emblems embroidered on their breast pocket. Billy finished his drink and approached the bar to ask the barman about the club he was due to meet. He pointed Billy towards the second group of men and his heart sank.

'It's those guys down there. Do you see the one with that chain of name bars hanging around his neck, looking like he's the mayor?' asked the barman, and without waiting for an answer to his rhetorical question continued. 'He's not the mayor – that's Pete.'

Billy remembered that Pete was the abrupt, angry voice on the phone, who had told him where the club met: 'The Coach and Horses, 7:30, next Tuesday.'

He took a deep breath in preparation, approached the group and introduced himself while making eye contact with Pete. Some shook his hand, some just smiled and nodded. Some didn't even break off from their conversation. About half the group didn't give him their names and those who did mumbled, so he didn't quite catch them amongst the background noise. Pete turned his head slightly to continue his discussion with his colleague, making Billy feel like he had interrupted.

'Do you want to get yourself a drink?' one of the members asked. 'We'll be going through in a moment.'

Eventually, Billy caught the barman's eye and ordered himself another drink. He turned around to find his group had disappeared and he had to ask the barman if he knew where they had gone. He pointed Billy in the direction of the rear of the property, through a door to an obviously unused 'function room' of the restaurant. The room was reserved for family gatherings, funerals and occasional parties, or at least it had been back in the day when the pub had been more popular.

Billy joined the men at their long table. There were about 15 men sitting around a long, slim rectangular table. He sat and listened for a while as they told stories of 'the old days' when the club was 'good'. They told jokes about events that had gone on and looked to Billy to approve by joining in with the laughter, which he did as politely as he could. At one point, one of the members turned to engage him in discussion.

'What do you do, then?'

'I'm a trainee manager at BCH on their graduate scheme.'

'I see, so you're a graduate are you? Done all the management training stuff, I suppose. Ambitious and career minded, I bet. A real go-getter headed for the stars, I would imagine. That's good. Good for you. You'd probably be too good for us.'

'Too good for us,' thought Billy. 'What does he mean by that, I wonder?'

'Reckon we can't teach you anything. Reckon you wouldn't gain anything from being a member of our club. We're all a bit old, too long in the tooth, a bit stayed and boring for a graduate like you. We've had loads of fellas like you visit us and not show up again.'

Shortly after this conversation, heads turned as a very gregarious character entered the function room.

'Good evening everyone,' boomed the rotund member. 'Sorry I'm late. You can start the meeting now I'm here,' he added, letting out a self-important laugh.

The member entered accompanied by another young underling, who looked positively traumatised by his attendance.

'Here, you sit here, Joe,' said the rotund bellower, as he pointed at the seat next to Billy. 'I've got to sit up that end next to the chairman because I'm the secretary,' and he headed off to the other end of the table with what Billy described as an air of arrogance mixed with pompous delusion of grandeur.

Billy suddenly felt confident comparing himself to his new compatriot. He struck up a quick rapport with Joe and established that this, too, was his first meeting.

Billy soon also established that another young man sitting nearby was a guest who was very enthusiastic about becoming a member. He was extolling the virtues of membership and sharing in infinite detail the events and activities he'd experienced since coming along as a guest.

Listening in were members who were courting the young man showing what appeared to be genuine interest in him. Having told the listeners about the eight meetings he'd attended, Billy asked a question.

'So when and how will you become a member?'

'I don't know,' the young man replied.

With this, one of the older members who had been listening intently intervened. 'Firstly, you must attend a minimum of six meetings, and once you have done that you will be assessed as to your suitability.'

Billy was flabbergasted, internally of course. This chap had already attended two more meetings than the minimum required and nobody had thought to mention the possibility of him becoming a full member.

'So where do you get your new members from?' Billy asked, as his confidence grew.

'Oh, you know, here and there. Members bring their friends and colleagues along. Once they come along once, they like it and come back and, eventually, become members.'

'How many members have you had join in the last two years?' enquired Billy.

'Erm, now let's see,' said the member, as he looked around the room. 'Erm, that's a good question. John was the last member to join. John! John!' he shouted down the table over everyone in between and, when John looked up, asked, 'When did you join?'

'About four years ago now.'

Billy began to question why Alex had ever sent him along to this club. Things only went from bad to worse as the evening wore on, with members arguing over how to spend some of the charity cash they had raised, with 'points of order' raised that resembled the debates he'd watched on TV from the Houses of Parliament. The night eventually came to a close past midnight. As Billy left the pub and headed towards the car park, he passed another public house, from which the first group of guys he'd seen in the Coach and Horses earlier were leaving. They were laughing, the energy was high and they all seemed to have had a relaxed, fun night. The pub looked newly refurbished with bright decor, sleek, modern furniture and wooden flooring. Billy would have described it as a 'yuppy pub'. He checked out the menu that included fresh, modern, tasty-sounding dishes – a complete contrast to the 'anything with chips' menu in the pub where he had spent the evening.

Billy headed for the car park and the drive home.

Now, I know as you read this, you may well be thinking, 'No way, there are no clubs out there like that.' Alas, there are clubs like the story depicts; I know this, because I write from my own experience. Scary, isn't it?

Or perhaps you will be thinking, 'Our club isn't like that.' Unfortunately, in some instances, the kind of experience that Billy describes may be described by some members as 'not happening in my club' when, in reality, it very much is.

Finally, you might be clenching your fists resolutely and saying, 'We must do everything possible to avoid being like that.' And that resolution, of course, is what will create the successful clubs in the future, the kind of clubs with the kind of members that will provide the good, strong society I truly wish for our communities.

In my experience, the clubs that are led by people who genuinely care about their members are those which generally flourish, grow and succeed.

As well as taking a good, hard look at yourself, and where you stand, and seeing that exactly as it is, there is also a need to take on board the views of how others see you. It's important to take this feedback constructively, not personally, and with the mind-set that 'their perception is my reality'.

If we take the way in which others see us and describe us as our reality, and we compare this to how we want to be perceived, we will gain an insight into whether we are walking our talk and are truly as we want to be.

Unfortunately, in my experience, many clubs and, in particular, members of clubs who do not see themselves as others see them struggle to acknowledge that change is necessary and, indeed, what change is necessary. This is usually as a result of pride muddying the waters, or the good old 'head in the sand' syndrome, also known as denial. Once a club recognises the differences between how they wish to be perceived and how they are portraying themselves, then the proverbial battle is half won.

I was involved with one organisation that undertook over a number of years at least three surveys. Some of what was reported was quite damning, some was very positive and a lot meant the public's perception was quite different to what the members knew to be the case. Some of the recommendations have been taken heed of and with positive impact.

This kind of survey is simply what the corporate world refers to as 'market research'. A fortune is spent in the corporate world on market research and not only for start-up businesses, product launches or rebrands, although these are key times when such measures are employed. Businesses who stay ahead of their competitors continually research their markets

KEY LEARNINGS

So how can a club find out how it is perceived compared to how it feels it wants to be seen? This is a very good question.

Corporate businesses spend a fortune on market research and, to date, I am yet to find an organisation that has budgets on such matters similar to their corporate counterparts. That said, the fact that the budget doesn't allow for such expensive market research should not deter clubs from copying big businesses, they just need to do so on a smaller, less expensive scale.

There are free internet-based survey software programmes available these days where simple questions can be asked of members and members can be encouraged to court the feedback of their own networks. Likewise, these can also be forwarded around members of the public via facilities such as social media websites.

Questionnaires can also be used to obtain information at events or when people are entering competitions or raffles, etc.

The thing to note here is that if the public at large think you are something different to what you believe you are, then there is a mismatch that will ultimately mean recruitment will be more difficult, as potential members' perceptions have to be corrected first. If, on the other hand, the public know you exactly as you are, neither better nor worse, then every member of the public can become a recruitment officer for you.

This is obviously two-fold. Firstly, you need to understand how others see you. Secondly, where there are differences, there must be a campaign of education to inform and correct any misunderstandings. This is best and mostly cheaply achieved through excellent PR via local press and internet presence. For instance, if the public think you are boring and staid, and you know yourself to be fun and vibrant, then ensure the photographs sent to the newspapers portray these aspects. Make sure your website is fun and vibrant. Make sure your members talk about their club in the same terms.

Another way to help is to bring on board ambassadors who may hold influential positions and come into contact with a lot of the public and who can help and assist you in getting the right message and correct persona portrayed. Some clubs have honorary positions, for instance. These could be the local editor of the local newspaper, a local estate agent, optician or dentist. If the club meets at a hotel or restaurant, invite the owner or manger to find out more about you by being a temporary or honorary member.

In my opinion, one thing is certain – most people do not and will not join a club or society without some knowledge or experience. More and more clubs offer first-meeting-free initiatives, try-before-you-buy events, or temporary membership. These are all aimed at encouraging an individual to make up their own mind first so they can choose what is right for them. What can you and your club offer prospective members?

Chapter Five
The Seven Mistakes

Chapter Five The Seven Mistakes

'How did you feel the next morning, Billy?' asked Alex, as he picked up his coffee cup to take a sip.

'Absolutely shattered.'

'Did you feel energised or deflated by the experience? Better or worse off as a result?'

'Deflated and feeling like I'd wasted my time,' answered Billy, now confident in speaking his true feelings. 'But I know you must have sent me there for a reason, Alex. What was it?'

'The purpose of that meeting was to highlight to you the mistakes that poor clubs make. The mistakes poor organisations make. The mistakes that poor leaders make.'

'There are seven categories I relate to, Billy, and all the mistakes fall into one category or another somehow. The first is "exclusivity". This is where outsiders are left feeling out in the cold. They are not made to feel welcome or part of the group from the beginning.'

'Unlike the other group of men in the bar who bought their guest a drink,'

called Billy.

'Precisely,' confirmed Alex.

'And the use of in jokes. Those members who didn't acknowledge me at the bar or introduce me to the members in turn.'

'That's it,' continued Alex. 'The next is "boring meetings".'

'You don't need to tell me. The discussions about £50 here and £100 there. This needy cause or that needy cause and, do you know what, they had £2000 in the account so could have supported both!'

'Hmm,' encouraged Alex. 'And what about their programme of events?'

'They shared their programme with us and it does seem a bit boring, the same format each time. They seem to do the same things each year too, so many of the older members don't bother going to some of the meetings because they've been there and done that.'

'Third up is "intro & go",' Alex hesitated to allow Billy to comment.

'That will be Joe. What a nice chap. In fact, I've arranged to meet him for a drink next week at a different pub in town.'

'That's good. Yes, but what do you mean?' asked Alex.

'The way he was brought in, told to sit down without being introduced to anyone and left to fend for himself. No wonder he looked terrified.'

'Number four is "poor language".'

'What do you mean by that?' quizzed Billy.

'You mentioned the members who talked about the "old days" when the club was strong and good, right?' queried Alex.

'Yes.'

'Well, if they are talking about when it *used to be* good,' claimed Alex, 'what does that imply they believe the club to be today?'

'Bad?' offered Billy.

'Exactly,' said Alex. 'You see, sometimes, people say things without thinking and those moments tell us more about them and about their perception than it does about what it is or who it is they are talking about.'

'Yes, I see. It doesn't sound too good, does it? Is that the same as the comment "You'd be too good for us"?' Billy was now thinking ahead.

'Kind of, but that is a great example of the next mistake. "Prejudice".'

'That's a harsh term,' challenged Billy.

'Maybe, but let's just look at its literal meaning – to prejudge a situation or event. Now, the member you spoke of prejudged you, your likes and dislikes, your motivations and whether you would even want to be a member of their club.'

'And I was a bit offended too, to be honest,' admitted Billy.

'I can understand that, Billy, but, remember, he wasn't doing it maliciously. He was only basing his thoughts on his previous experiences. There are a lot of people in the world who prejudge other people's response to avoid the risk of rejection and, in doing so, don't allow individuals to decide for themselves.'

'I see,' said Billy. 'What's next?' Billy was getting excited at just how much he had learned from one night out, and it was fast becoming apparent that it had not been such a waste of time after all.

'Number six,' obliged Alex, 'is "complacency" – the art of not getting in first, sitting back and waiting for others to take the initiative that so often results in poor or zero results. It is very similar to inaction.'

'Like the way their members come from groups of friends or colleagues, but that they just seem to turn up almost unbeknown to most of the members?' suggested Billy.

'Correct.'

'The member I spoke to about this had never introduced a member himself. In fact, he had never even invited anyone as a guest. When I asked why, he said it was because what the club offered was just boring dinner meetings but it was a chance to get out of the house. If his friends or colleagues knew what a boring club he was a member of, his reputation would be, to use his words, "through the floor".' Billy then went on, 'Is that also like the guest who had been along to lots of meetings, but had not yet been asked to join?'

'Not quite,' offered Alex. 'I call this "not listening" because the situation you described was the guest explaining everything he'd done as a guest, then the member having not listened offered advice that was either inappropriate, out of context or just contradictory to the experience being relayed. He had simply not listened and alienated the guest as a result.'

'I see.'

The two agreed the visit had not been such a waste of time as Billy had first thought. They finished their coffees and this time Billy paid the waiter, 'Thank you, Archie.'

As they walked across the square, they arranged to meet again the following week.

'You will do well to remember the mistakes you have observed, Billy. If you do nothing else but avoid them yourself, you will be a good leader. To be a great leader, however, you need to know what to do instead of making those mistakes.'

'Is that the four elements of great leadership?'

'Yes, it is. But, first, you need to understand the building jigsaws principle and about doing sums.'

I am sure we can all recall witnessing, experiencing or being a part of one or more of the seven mistakes. These points are not raised to say one thing is right or wrong, but merely to raise awareness of the things that can be perceived by our guests and prospective members as being a turn-off. The idea of raising awareness is so that we can look out for them and, hopefully, avoid them in our clubs moving forward.

I once addressed a conference during which a delegate related that they had been party to a debate about all the things that go wrong in clubs, based on the experience of those taking part. After a short discussion, it was concluded that in fact many of the examples they had highlighted could be grouped together and fitted into one of these seven categories. I believe that any example of poor recruitment and retention behaviour falls specifically or loosely into one of the following:

Exclusivity
There is nothing more off-putting for a prospective member than to be ignored or excluded from what is going on.

I have known a prospective member to be sent to the wrong venue in error and, instead of one of the members going in person to meet them, apologise and make sure they felt welcomed, they were just called and told 'you're in the wrong place'. Not a particularly warm welcome I'm sure you'd agree.

Boring meetings
Have you ever sat through a long drawn-out meeting where the matter being debated could have been dealt with in a far more concise manner? Many of us have, I am sure.

If the mantra of 'why use seven words when only 7000 will do' exists in your club, whether as a group or an individual, then this needs to be addressed because one factor that is the biggest barrier to most prospective members is they are time-poor.

Time is the one commodity we do not have enough of, we cannot buy and, therefore, I refer to it as the most precious commodity for our members. We must ensure their time spent with us is spent very wisely. For most people, listening to the same debate with the same point being made by numerous people constitutes a waste of their time.

Intro & go

Billy witnessed a classic case of Intro & go, and there are a number of ways that Intro & go manifests itself:

- Guests left to fend for themselves during pre-meeting or meal drinks.
- Guests left to fend for themselves after the meeting or meal.
- Guests who become members and are later abandoned in favour of other new guests.
- New members who, in their enthusiasm for all things new, are left to attend events or represent the club on their own for a number of reasons. This can be pretty lonely.

I know of clubs that have not long since inducted a member to be discussing with them the possibility of them being the leader/chair/president, etc. This can turn new members off and fill them with dread.

In brief, guests, new members and existing members who are stepping up all need to feel supported not abandoned.

Poor language

Remember, it is not just *what* is said but also *how* it is said that has an impact on the listener. If you have members who moan and groan about how the club is run, what the club gets up to or club decisions, then they are undermining the foundation of the club to be able to recruit new members. Any negative talk has to be eradicated. This doesn't mean all members need to be happy-clappy all the time. However, there are ways to be respectful and constructive that do not have a negative impact on others.

Prejudice

Some clubs go out of their way to select who they consider to be the right people in order to invite them to be members. There is a counter argument that says invite lots of people to become members and, if the club is good and strong, the club will be the making of the person. This may mean a low conversion rate, but it is a numbers game. Ten per cent of 100 introduced guests being retained as members is better than a 50 per cent retention rate of ten carefully selected individuals.

By far, the former selection process is usually a more laborious, time-consuming process. It can, and often does, have a negative impact on morale, as lots of time and effort is put into a small number of people who feel the pressure to join and, if they choose not to, the members investing in those guests can easily lose motivation.

There is a balance to be struck to ensure guests and club are well suited and that any recruitment process being employed is not too onerous or time restrictive.

From experience, I would recommend never prejudging a character. You will invariably be surprised – sometimes pleasantly, sometimes disappointingly. Slow down your decision-making process and let the personality be revealed.

Complacency

In a world that is continually changing, improving, progressing and developing, if we stand still, we will regress. There used to be a well-known principle in marketing terms that a potential customer needed to be nudged, hear about or see an advert seven times before becoming aware of the existence of the advertiser. It is now widely understood that the number of nudges, listens or sightings has now increased to 12.

With the massive increase in membership organisations all wanting a piece of their members' disposable income and their disposable time, the competition for members has increased dramatically. Therefore, sitting back and waiting is no longer a strategy that will see clubs and societies continue to grow successfully. The clubs and organisations that have had recent success have embraced the changes in the world and changed how they recruit. They have realised that what used to work 10, 20 or 50 years ago does not apply today.

Not listening

This is a trait that will almost certainly always end in the death knell being rung for any organisation, club or society.

All groups must continually listen to their members. This includes their old members and their new members. They must listen to their guests, prospective members and members of the public who have no awareness of their existence.

A club that stops listening is one that has stopped communicating and, like it or not, we now live in a communication age with communication at the heart of all that we do.

People who are natural 'belongers' want to be part of something that gives them access to others with a similar interest, with a like-mind, and others with whom they can engage. If the club, the organisation or the individuals forget this, they will be closing their club rather than expanding it. Engagement requires communication and this is a two-way process.

KEY LEARNINGS

The purpose of this book is to, firstly, make you aware of these mistakes so you can spot them happening. Secondly, once you spot them happening, the next step is to stop them happening and, thirdly, to replace those behaviours with new better ways of doing things.

This book sets out some answers that have been found to work for other organisations, clubs and individuals, and so may well work for you too. Or, of course, may inspire an answer to be found that hasn't been suggested.

At this stage the seven mistakes should be acknowledged and a promise made to stop making them. If you were to stop reading this book at this point (and I sincerely hope you don't), then, if nothing else, stopping these behaviours alone will have a positive impact on any club.

- Exclusivity: Stop it happening now.
- Boring meetings: Stop them happening now.
- Intro & go: Stop it happening now.
- Poor language: Stop it happening now.
- Prejudice: Stop it happening now.
- Complacency: Stop it happening now.
- Not listening: Stop it happening now.

Once the behaviours have been acknowledged and a commitment made to stop them happening, we are in a place where we are ready to consider replacing those behaviours with new, more constructive and more effective behaviours. These are set out in the rest of this book.

Chapter Six

Doing Sums and
Building Jigsaws

Chapter Six Doing Sums and Building Jigsaws

'Hello again, sir,' Archie welcomed Billy to his square-side café.

'Hi, Archie,' replied Billy enthusiastically, excited about meeting Alex again to learn more. 'Two coffees please, Archie. Alex will be here any moment.'

Archie disappeared into the café property and almost immediately Alex appeared. 'Hello, Billy. How's your week been?' Alex was impressed with Billy's enthusiasm and keenness arriving ahead of time.

Billy was telling Alex about his week, his reflections of the seven mistakes he had observed and about how he had caught himself making them himself during the week. He had stopped himself immediately and changed what he was doing for something more positive.

'That's excellent, Billy,' commended Alex. 'How did that feel?'

'A bit strange. As we talked about the mistakes last week, I kept thinking to myself, but I don't do that anyway so I'm okay. But now I realise I did and that I needed to change some of my habits.'

'How does the thought of change sit with you?' probed Alex.

'I'm really not sure,' started Billy. 'I've heard a lot of people express that they don't like change, they like things just the way they are, they don't want managers coming in and changing things, messing up their routines.'

'That's very true, many people don't like change. Change management is a big part of being a great leader. When a leader is thrust into a new role, they have to accept that they are not only part of the change process but also, for many of their new team, the catalyst for change. Great leaders understand the principle that change is not about changing circles into squares; it's about developing circles into spheres. It then forms the platform from which those spheres can be launched into orbit.'

'Your coffee, sir,' Archie placed the first cup in front of Alex as he always did. 'And yours, sir,' he added, as he set the second cup down in front of Billy.

'Thank you, Archie,' Billy smiled.

Alex smiled to himself knowing that Billy had thoughtfully placed an order for both coffees on his arrival. Archie had even more thoughtfully held the order back until he had arrived; making Billy look efficient and making sure Alex's coffee was served piping hot.

'You were going to share the jigsaw principle with me today,' blurted out Billy in his excitement.

'Yes,' Alex said, as he took his cup from his mouth following his first sip of coffee. 'When you are building a jigsaw, tell me, what are the first pieces you find?'

Billy thought for a moment, 'The four corners?' he asked.

'Yes, good. And how do you know they are the four corner pieces?'

'They have two flat sides?' Billy stated in the form of a question giving away his lack of confidence in his answer.

'Yes, that's right,' said Alex. 'They are the only four pieces in the box that have two flat sides. Tell me, Billy. At this point, are you able to see the whole picture?'

Billy thought for a moment, 'No,' he said.

'Correct, so we've made a start. We have our corners in place, yet we are unable to see the whole picture. Good. So, what do you do next?'

'Look out the straight-edged pieces and build the edge,' Billy answered, pleased with his ability to know the answer.

'Why do you do that?'

'Because all those pieces are unique as they have one flat side.'

'So why is that stage so important?' probed Alex.

Billy thought for a while and eventually conceded, 'I don't know.'

'Okay,' began Alex. 'The thing is, once you have the perimeter mapped out you know that every other piece fits inside there somewhere, doesn't it?' Being a rhetorical question, Alex continued. 'You see, at this stage you do not know exactly where each piece fits, but you have at least narrowed down the options. At this point, Billy, tell me, are you able to see the whole picture?'

'Erm,' Billy hesitated for a while, thought and wondered where this line of questioning was going, 'No.' This time his answer was more quizzical than certain.

'Right again,' said Alex. 'We have now made significant progress. We have created our boundary, we know that every piece fits inside that boundary and yet we are still unable to see the big picture. Okay, so what do you do next?'

Billy's thoughts flew back to the building of the jigsaw and not on the line of questioning. 'Pick out pieces of similar colours and begin to randomly slot them together.'

'That's good. So, you may now have a few clusters of pieces, some no doubt inside the perimeter and some may even have been built outside the perimeter.' Billy nodded his approval. 'So, at this stage, are you able to see the whole picture?'

'No,' answered Billy, more confidently than last time.

'Correct. We have worked now on the detail of some parts of the puzzle, sometimes in great detail and, yet, while having a very good image of a small part of the big picture, we have worked on those small areas in isolation to other areas. If we stand back, we still don't see the whole picture. We may even have parts of the puzzle that we have worked on tirelessly, yet they remain outside of the boundary because we can't quite work out where they fit in yet.' Alex was a master at developing metaphors without having to explain their meanings. He allowed his students to discover their own parallels from his metaphors and, in doing so, experience their own learning rather than being told the answers.

'Let's now roll the clock forward a while,' Alex continued. 'You have virtually completed your 1000 piece jigsaw, but there are a few pieces missing. They are not in the box or remaining on the table. They've obviously been misplaced for the moment. Let's say, out of 1000 pieces there are 20 pieces missing, randomly spaced around the puzzle. Do you now see enough of the picture to make out the whole?'

'Yes, I guess so.'

'Correct. Billy, this is the point during the process where we will build a jigsaw together. Sometimes we may focus on one part of the jigsaw puzzle and you may not know where it fits in okay?' Billy nodded. 'On other occasions, we will build other parts of the puzzle that may look completely different. Just know they are all parts of the same jigsaw and, eventually, you will see the effect of the sum of all the small pieces creating a detailed picture.'

'I see,' smiled Billy, as he began to understand the metaphor again.

'When we have completed our work there may be a few pieces missing, but we must avoid getting bogged down worrying about those few missing pieces. They will turn up at some later stage – they always do.'

In his usual enthusiastically impatient way Billy asked, 'Which are the first pieces of the jigsaw then?' pleased with himself that he was able to talk in the language of the metaphor.

'The four corners. The pieces from which all other pieces hang,' replied Alex.

'The four foundation stones of great leadership?' Billy asked, again pleased he had begun to piece his own puzzle together.

'That's right,' said Alex. 'But before we look at those elements in detail, we need to understand the concept of doing sums. It helps us to see things in simple terms.'

'But I was never very good at maths in school,' confessed Billy.

'Precisely, not many people are or were. Not many people enjoy maths. They get confused with the complex equations, algebra and all the different formulae.'

'Yes, that was me.'

'I enjoyed maths, though. And I put it down to my teacher in high school. He was one of those inspirational teachers, you know? It's amazing, isn't it, how sometimes you meet people or people come into your life and they inspire you or give you a message?'

'A hidden gem?' Billy remembered an earlier conversation.

'Exactly. They give you a hidden gem – something that you only get the real value of later on with reflection or hindsight. Well, my maths teacher, Mr Vincent, was certainly one of those characters. I wasn't the most successful of academic students in my year, or indeed my school, but I was okay in maths, thanks to Mr Vincent being able to unlock the potential in me. I'm sure he did it for a great number of students, probably some of them went on to great mathematical success as a direct result.'

'How did he do that?' Billy was now intrigued.

'I'll never forget that first maths lesson. Like all apprehensive expectant school kids all across the world, we sat there in the classroom waiting for the teacher to arrive at the start of the new school year, in a new school. Mr Vincent walked in and I'll always remember his opening welcoming words: "So why are you all here?" "To do maths, sir!" we replied. "No, forget that. We will not be doing maths for the next two years. We'll be doing *sums!*" When the laughter subsided, he continued. "Yes, we'll be doing sums. You can all already do sums can't you? You know adding up, taking away, multiplication and division?" There was still some tittering and sniggering at the back of the class. "You see maths is just lots of sums done in particular sequences. All we will do is lots of sums – sums that you can already do." It was like a lightbulb moment for me,' Alex continued. 'Here was a man who masterfully took a complex subject and broke it down into its simplest components and made it easy right from the start. One day I'm sure you will hear about the Johari Window. Mr

Vincent really opened up the arena that day.'

'Wow, no wonder you were inspired by him.'

'And many more besides me,' Alex mused. 'He's inspired people he's never even met through me and maybe others too. You see, it's an art form taking something complex and simplifying it into its component parts, breaking it down into simple, easy manageable steps, steps which, on their own, just about anyone can perform. There are only four component elements in maths and once you have mastered those you can find the solution to any problem. You just have to find the right sequence. You see the significance to great leadership?'

'I certainly do,' said Billy.

'I shared the story once with a mathematician whom I met at a seminar. He was touched by the story and I could tell in his eyes it started another chain of thought. The next day, he came looking for me during one of the breaks. 'You know that story of your maths teacher,' he said. 'You can take it even one step further. There are in fact only two component steps in maths – addition and subtraction. Multiplication is just an extension of addition and division an extension of subtraction. Anyway, my real reason for finding you was to ask you, do you think your teacher would mind if I used his concept to help me inspire my students?' I told him I was sure he'd be delighted. You know, he was a university lecturer, Billy.'

'Incredible.'

'Great leadership is made up of four component parts and by mastering them we will be able to solve any problem that faces us, and that is what great leadership is all about.'

'Your bill, sir,' said Archie, with impeccable timing as ever.

'Thank you, Archie,' Alex acknowledged. 'I'll get this,' he turned to Billy. 'You can get next week's when you get an introduction to the first component – greatness.'

'Any darn fool can make something complex; it takes a genius to make something simple.' *Albert Einstein*

I was fortunate to work with one organisation while it was undergoing a review of its structure, how it operated and how it was governed. The first thing that was done was to consult the membership on what direction they wanted to see the organisation take, and to set out the vision of the organisation. This provided understanding and clarity from both perspectives.

From here, the goals of the project were agreed, with clarity on how those factors would be measured. Collectively, all also agreed what results would constitute success.

Then, and only then, came the detail of how those steps would be implemented. This helped the organisation to stay on track and maintained the focus of the members to stay true to the process in hand. Each step was broken down piece by piece. Sometimes work was done in infinite detail in one area, without any concern for how this may 'fit in' with other areas of the big picture. This work was done with an understanding and collective belief and trust that by the end of the process the picture would be visible.

There was a conscious stream of creativity, review and prioritisation before action. A collaborative approach to the prioritisation meant that all members were involved and agreed to each step along the way. They all understood the big picture, shared in its building or painting and, even when they may not have agreed personally, adopted an adult mind of accepting the views of the majority in the name of success.

The outcome has been the production of a long-term strategy, an understanding by all of the strategy, what the end result of success will look like and the delivery of the strategy to produce those results.

For instance, it was identified that one of the areas the organisation struggled with was a consistent approach to dealing with membership enquiries across all their local clubs. Local branches dealt with enquiries differently, whether they were passed to them from central office, they were received in person, via their website or from a lead generating initiative of some sort. It was agreed that the fundamental steps to follow for successful conversion of enquiry to recruitment at local branch level were:

Receive enquiry > Make contact > Discuss forthcoming events > Decide event/date > Make arrangements > Attend meeting

However, how a club collectively goes about such a process may overcomplicate matters. For example, if the chair receiving the enquiry by email sends out an email to all members saying, 'I've had this enquiry, will someone get in touch?', this may only deliver a response of apathy. All members may sit back and wait for someone else in the club to volunteer. The end result is nothing happens.

Great clubs have a structured process and a clearly defined structure of who is responsible for doing what, and how their bit of the process helps achieve the end result successfully. This is set out and agreed in advance, with roles defined, understood and clear.

- Enquiry – all enquiries are directed to the membership team leader, not the chair.
- Membership team leader – acknowledges receipt, introduces themselves, asks for most effective means of contact, i.e. asks for a phone number.
- Membership team leader delegates to a membership team member, with phone number or email (if no number is forthcoming).
- Membership team member makes contact – following the agreed consistent protocol – introduces themselves, ascertains the reason for their enquiry, explains a little of what the club is about, quantifies the interest, shares forthcoming events and/or meetings, asks which will be most suitable for them to attend, confirms details.

- Membership team member then reports back to the chair and membership team leader with the details of the guest attending agreed meeting.
- Membership team leader notifies all members of the club about the guest ahead of the meeting, sharing name and details of the guest so all members can make them feel welcome.

Once these steps have been agreed and all members know who is responsible for which parts of the process, each can take responsibility for their part and deliver in an agreed manner.

Each stage of the process can be looked at in detail independently to the other stages in the process, knowing where it 'fits in', so that a step-by-step guide can be formulated. This may seem overly complex for a small club, however, the simplicity of the process being broken down means any individual can follow the steps set out without 'training' or prior knowledge easily and, most importantly, consistently for the enquirer.

KEY LEARNINGS

In order to grow membership, most organisations decide they must market themselves better, increase their profile and build awareness of their existence. However, this is 'forward planning' not 'backward planning'.

If a club is going to increase its membership, it must first ensure it has the ability to induct increased numbers of members, otherwise it may find it creates bad experiences rather than good ones for their prospective members. So, for any club embarking on a recruitment campaign, it must first have the infrastructure in place to cope with an increase in enquiries, the ability to host guests at meetings and welcome new members.

Some organisations may have restrictions. As an example, take London City Livery Companies, which have an upper limit of the number of Liverymen that may be clothed at any one time. Also, private golf clubs which have a maximum number of members/voters/shareholders as part of their constitution. Consider a children's club that requires a maximum number of children per supervising adult and so their 'membership' is restricted by the number of supervising adults they have available to them. There is no point in driving more enquiries through the door if they cannot be accommodated.

Lots of organisations rely heavily on volunteers from within its membership. However, many of these organisations do not provide the necessary framework to support and guide individuals on how to recruit well. Lots of organisations are great at giving their members means and ways, procedures, processes and step-by-step guidance on how to raise money, organise events, raise awareness, etc., but few offer their members the same level of support in how to recruit.

In my experience, many clubs do not advise their members that they are 'allowed' to recruit. They neither tell them how to recruit nor give them guidelines on how to recruit effectively. Recruitment, therefore, often becomes the function of the membership team within an organisation, instead of utilising the greater resource of all its members, to recruit and then handover to the membership team.

Great recruitment organisations make it part of their DNA to recruit, and to recruit very early on within an individual's membership. Networking clubs and organisations, especially commercially-run versions, are great at setting out from the outset that members are required to recruit new members each year, for instance. This maintains freshness in the network and maintains a vibrancy in the club.

Chapter Seven

Archie's Story

Chapter Seven Archie's Story

Billy got to the café a couple of minutes early as had become his habit. As he approached, he noticed the café was quieter than normal. He sat down at the table that he had come to accept as 'his'.

'Can I get you anything?' came an unfamiliar voice over his shoulder, which made him turn around to see who had approached him.

'Thank you,' he began, as his heart sank a little. Before him was another waiter, dressed the same as Archie but not quite as pristine as Archie. The new waiter seemed less confident, less comfortable in his role and did not seem as relaxed and happy as Billy had come to expect from 'his' waiter. There was a different atmosphere today. Although the sun shone, it felt cold, clinical and sterile.

Billy had begun to expect Archie's attention and his concern rose, 'Is Archie okay? Is he off sick?'

'No, he's just having a day off,' came the matter-of-fact retort. 'I'm normally in the kitchen.'

Billy ordered two coffees and smiled to himself as he wondered why this waiter was normally kept in the kitchen while Archie was left to wait on tables. He also wondered if the quietness of the café was as a direct consequence of Archie's absence.

'Here you go,' said the new waiter, within what seemed like seconds. 'And there's the bill,' he placed the slip on the table and slid one of the coffees on top of it to stop it blowing away. Billy noticed that some of the coffee slopped into the saucer.

Billy carefully swapped the coffees so that when his guest arrived he was not greeted with the dirty saucer. Billy enjoyed people watching and, as he sat sipping his coffee, he watched the world go by.

After a rather uncharacteristic delay in Alex's appearance Billy started to wonder if he had somehow got the day wrong. He was just about to finish his coffee when another young man approached his table.

'Hello, Billy.'

'Hello, Archie,' Billy was a bit startled to see his favourite waiter standing at his table in jeans and a T-shirt rather than his usual pristine uniform. 'I hear you have the day off?'

'Yes, I'm sorry I'm late,' Archie began to sit down at the table with Billy.

'I'm sorry,' started Billy. 'You're late? I'm confused.'

'Alex called me yesterday to say that he was unable to make your regular meeting today, and asked if I might like to meet with you instead. As I had nothing else to do, I accepted his invitation.'

'Great.' Billy caught the replacement waiter's eye as he busied himself pottering at the waiter's station. 'Let me get you a drink.'

'Thank you,' Archie said to Billy, then turned to look at the waiter as he got to the table. 'Can I have a cup of tea, please?'

'And may I have another cup of coffee, please?' Billy asked, noting the original second cup had now gone cold.

The waiter said nothing. He looked at the full coffee cup in the middle of the table, wrote on his pad and turned to head to the kitchen.

The two exchanged small talk and discussed how Billy knew Alex. Archie told of the numerous young managers and graduates whom Alex had brought to his café over the years he had been working there. They chatted about what Billy had learned in the few weeks he'd been working with Alex on his development programme towards great leadership. They discussed the stepping stones and stream incident, the jigsaw, his visit to the club and about Mr Vincent.

'Here you are,' the waiter said, delivering the drinks. He then picked up the original coffee cup, placed a second bill on top of the first and replaced the cup and saucer back on top of them, spilling yet more coffee into the saucer.

'That school teacher story reminds me of a story my father used to tell me,' said Archie.

Billy had begun to trust his instinct and, remembering he had two ears, decided to see if he was about to discover another hidden gem, 'Yes? Go on,' he beckoned.

'One day, I was called to the head mistress's office. My heart sank, I wondered what I had done wrong. My tummy churned as I walked the long corridor to her office. I was only about five or six years old and had only been going to proper school for about a year. I had already learned, though, that being called to the head mistress's office probably meant trouble.'

Billy began to think back to the times he had been summoned to a head teacher's office and empathised with Archie.

Archie went on to describe the head mistress's office, the large chair he was asked to sit in and how she peered over her glasses at him.

'I've been talking to some of the teachers,' the head mistress explained to Archie. 'We've been discussing your work and your relationships with some of the other children,' she continued. 'And we'd like to know what's behind your behaviour.'

*****

While Archie's mum was preparing the family dinner that night, Archie heard his parents talking.

'When I got to the school gate tonight,' said his dad, 'Archie's head mistress approached me.'

Archie was in the dining room while his parents were in the kitchen and was trying hard to listen in to what was being discussed.

'She asked me to accompany her to her office. She said that she and some of the other teachers had been discussing Archie's performance and his relationships with other kids in his class. Archie's performance is significantly different to others of his age. I was really concerned,' Archie's dad admitted. 'My heart was racing and my hands were sweating. She went on to say Archie's performance was exceptional. When he is set a task, he just gets on with it until it is complete. He always works hard. He is always polite and always smiling. He never complains about work. While he is not the top of the class, he always performs consistently without off-days and outperforms his abilities. The other kids argue to sit next to him in class and they fight to play with him during playtimes. She says he's an outstanding individual and that they'd like to share whatever it is that Archie has with other kids. That's why they spoke with him.'

'Wow, that's amazing,' said Archie's mum.

'The head mistress said that she had spoken with Archie and he said it's down to me. When she asked him what he meant he said it's because I ask him two questions every morning as I finish my breakfast and leave for work.'

'Do you?' enquired Archie's mum.

'Yes, I do, but I didn't realise…' Archie's dad's sentence was interrupted by Archie walking into the kitchen.

'So, what are these two questions your dad asks you each morning, Archie?' asked his mum in a loving, warm, motherly, reassuring way, that let him realise he was not in trouble – quite the opposite.

Archie looked up at his dad, who had pride etched on his face.

*****

Archie recounted for Billy those mornings over breakfast and re-enacted the dialogue that his mother had witnessed for the first time all those years ago. 'What kind of a day are you going to have today, Archie?' 'A great day, Dad.' 'And who is responsible for that, Archie?' 'I am, Dad.'

'What did your mum say?' asked Billy.

'She didn't say anything. She just hugged me and my dad. You know, I still ask myself those same questions today in the mirror every morning before I leave home.'

Billy was not surprised to hear that last comment.

'Oh, I nearly forgot. Talking of having great days, Alex asked me to pass on his apologies for not being able to make it today, but asked if you'd meet him here next week at the same time.'

I have shared this story numerous times from stages and podiums and probably the funniest real-life example of this happened to me personally.

It was the morning of the largest speaking engagement I had so far been invited to. I had those 'big day' excitement feelings in my stomach that lets me know I'm going to have a great day. I was getting dressed and feeling pretty good about myself as I lifted out of the hotel wardrobe my specially selected brand-new suit, shirt, tie and shoes that made me feel like a million dollars. I pulled on my shirt only to find it was a little 'snug'. In fact, it was more than snug, and I was unable to button my collar.

My mood changed. I was beginning to feel a little less happy and a bit annoyed. I started to question what kind of a day I was going to have. My mood dropped further still when I took off my shirt and noticed that the collar size that should have been '18' read '16'. The label was quite small and the printing on the label was such that, in all honesty, it was easy to see how the six could have been mistaken for an eight. However, I was not in a forgiving mood. I was ready to lash out at anyone I could blame: my wife should have noticed when she washed and ironed my shirt; the shop assistant should have been more careful when selecting the shirt from the shelf. Of course, like many in those moments, I didn't stop for a moment to question whether I had checked the shirt when it was bought, or tried it on for size before having it washed and ironed. I certainly didn't question why I hadn't carried a second shirt with me to the hotel in case of any mishap.

I was fully into my blame game when a knock on the door interrupted me. It was my brother who often attended big events with me as my confidant and chief critic. He knew my material as well as I did. He sensed the tension immediately and asked what was wrong. I told him with the usual punctuation of blame and finger pointing. Then, once I had explained everything to him and got it all off my chest, he looked me square in the eye and said, 'Okay, so what kind of a day are you going to have?' and, after a short pause, 'And who is responsible for that?' It broke the mood perfectly; we both fell about laughing and came to the conclusion we'd never travel without a reserve shirt in future. We also agreed a solution to the immediate problem.

I later bound on to the stage, shirt buttons pulling like they were about to burst like on The Incredible Hulk's shirt when he got angry. Fortunately, my jacket was buttoned to hide most of the embarrassment beneath. I apologised to the audience for the fact I was not wearing a tie (as, being a traditionalist, I am never comfortable wearing a tie with an unfastened top button) and go on to tell them Archie's story to set the scene for the day.

Later in the day, I needed to remove my jacket for an exercise with the audience so I explained the sequence of events I encountered that morning. I reaffirmed that we all have learning experiences every day and asked the ladies to prepare themselves for a Hulk-like revelation as I removed my jacket. The audience laughed and laughed. It was one of the funniest moments of the day and many delegates came and said that they thought it was brilliant that I had deliberately worn a small shirt to emphasise the power of Archie's story. If only!

KEY LEARNINGS

I will often ask an audience how they are feeling and often get the response that they are 'okay', 'alright' or 'not bad'.

I have developed the notion that inside our heads live a number of little men and/or women. It's akin to the comic strip story I used to read as a child growing up in *Topper* and *Dandy* called 'The Numbskulls'. These numbskulls do as they are told, quite literally. They know how to create your mood and change your behaviour to deliver what it is you ask them to do.

For instance, if when asked how you are you answer 'I'm tired,' your numbskulls would push the buttons, pull the levers and twist the dials inside your head to make those wishes become a reality.

Imagine the difference, therefore, if when asked the same question you answer 'I could do with some more energy, to be honest'. What reaction might that get from your numbskulls?

We need to be careful with the language we use for ourselves, on ourselves and about ourselves. Our numbskulls hear every word, thought and wish made and, therefore, our numbskulls take action on all those words we utter and thoughts we have. People who when asked how they are reply with 'okay,' 'not bad' and 'alright' are, at best, setting themselves up for a non-descript day.

I recently heard an amazing story of a club that had been in membership decline. They were down to very low numbers so they decided that one of their strategies for growth was to put the word 'Mighty' in front of their name. In a matter of just a couple of years, that club has gone from verging on closure to growing membership and is now a strong club. So what word could you add to the front of your club name that might evoke a sense of strength and growth?

This chapter would not be complete without asking you the following:

- What kind of day are you going to have today or tomorrow?
- What kind of week are you going to have?
- What kind of month are you going to have?
- What kind of quarter are you going to have?
- What kind of year are you going to have?
- And, finally, most importantly – who is responsible for that?

Chapter Eight

Rubber Rings and Scales

Chapter Eight Rubber Rings and Scales

'What kind of a day are you going to have today, Archie?' 'A great day, Dad.' 'And who is responsible for that, Archie?' 'I am, Dad,' Billy shared with Alex the previous week's discussion he'd had with Archie.

'Good evening, sir,' Archie appeared at the table. 'The usual two coffees?' This time, Archie made eye contact with Billy while addressing them both for the first time.

'Yes please, thank you. What kind of a day have you had today, Archie?' 'A great day of course, sir,' Archie smiled. 'Thank you for asking.'

'Isn't that amazing?' asked Billy, turning to Alex as Archie headed back into the main building.

'Yes, it is Billy,' replied Alex. 'And that is the first element of greatness – taking care of and responsibility for your own greatness.'

Billy realised that Alex had deliberately conjured up what he thought had been a chance meeting between himself and Archie. 'Or was it?' he thought to himself. He was too discreet to ask and it didn't matter anyway. What he knew for certain was he was inspired by Archie's story, had complete respect for Alex and his way of teaching and admiration for Archie who so obviously walked his talk. Billy was enthralled and excited about what was to come. Despite knowing he had already learned a lot, and getting a sense that he had already come quite a distance in this particular expedition, he felt his journey into the four main elements of his desired learning was about to begin for real. He felt on the edge of something truly great.

'The next phase of greatness is to respect that others are in control of their own greatness and it is not under our control,' continued Alex. 'A mentor of mine once told me that it is not the job of a leader to motivate others.' Billy thought about how great the person who Alex referred to as his mentor must be. 'Great leaders recognise that it is their job to create the environment where others are self-motivated.'

Billy thought about that concept and Alex allowed him the time to digest what he'd just shared with him.

'So, if you have a team where you or someone in the team or a number of people in that team are choosing to be less great than they are capable of, or than you want or need them to be, how do you create the environment where they will improve?' enquired Billy.

'That's a great question and a well-worded one.' Alex appreciated Billy's ability to take on board his learning so quickly and to demonstrate this by speaking in the same terms Alex used, and state them positively. 'The answer to this holds the key to the difference between mediocre and great teams. I am often asked, "I am in a team where some people have great attitudes and others frankly stink, how do you deal with them?" and I am sure you can relate to this or a similar situation, can't you Billy?'

'Yes, I can,' said Billy, confidently.

Alex went on to introduce the concept of the 'Scale of one to ten' – a superb tool for eliciting measurement, removing ambiguity and gaining perspective.

Alex explained that some people measure things and relate to things in different ways: for instance, one person may consider a piece of work to be worthy of a score of three out of ten, while another may consider the same piece of work to be worthy of a much higher score. Imagine a local football team who wins every match in their league three years back-to-back, winning all the trophies. It would be expected that the players, the team and the supporters consider their achievement to be a ten out of ten. However, an individual in that team who wanted to make it big in the Premiership, may compare themselves to Premiership players and, therefore, score their performance according to those aspirations rather than limit them to the team and the league.

Sometimes people use imprecise language to try to describe experiences, for instance, and they will be using their own frames of reference for this. As an example, imagine a keen angler who, to date, has only ever caught a 5lb fish. When finally catching a 10lb fish, he would describe this latest catch as huge, massive or enormous. Whereas an angler who regularly catches 20lb fish may describe that same catch as a tiddler, tiny or bait.

The greatest thing about scales is it allows an insight into the world of the person; it allows perspective from their side and it allows us to set a frame of reference in order to obtain clarity. So, in the football scenario above, the individual footballer who may say he's a rubbish footballer may be encouraged to score his performance in relation to the rest of the team on a scale of one to ten, where one is the worst player and ten the best – giving himself a score of nine. Compared to the rest of the league, he may rate himself seven and, compared to all players including Premiership players in the whole country, he may class himself as five. You would probably agree this is far from 'rubbish' and often helps not only the coach to gain perspective but also the coachee.

Likewise, the angler may enthuse about his catch, yet on the scale of the size of that particular breed of fish ever caught he may score it a four, with his best previously being a two.

Alex then went on to set a scene where a person is in a team of ten, with mixed attitudes and a mixed level of chosen greatness. In the hypothetical scenario there are ten people, and each person's attitude is graded from one to ten, where ten is outstanding and one is a massive underachievement.

'Imagine if you will, Billy,' Alex went on, 'that there is one person in your team standing at each grade on the scale.'

'Yes,' again Billy was beginning to wonder where this was going, but had begun to trust that every time he experienced confusion it was soon followed by a learning experience.

'Most leaders spend their time, effort and energy trying to influence and change the views and behaviours of those at the bottom end of the scale. The problem with this is that those people take the most amount of time, effort and energy and often have the highest degrees of resistance to change. They are also the cause for most leaders giving up, failing or changing jobs.

'Change from circles to squares or circles to spheres?' asked Billy.

'All change, whether the individuals understand the change or not, perceive the change or not, or want the change or not, is from circles to spheres. The degrees of resistance can be enough to eventually defeat even the strongest of leaders. What great leaders recognise as a better way to create a great environment of great self-motivation is first to lead by example. Then they nurture and empower those near the top of the scale. So, for instance, a person originally standing at a nine makes the small move up to a ten.'

'I guess they are more likely to be responsive to development too, aren't they?' asked Billy.

'They are indeed,' Alex continued. 'Once someone moves off the number nine spot there is now a gap that is left, a void, if you will, or a vacuum. This vacuum, then draws in those around it, so the person standing at eight has a place to move to and can be encouraged with a bit of time and effort to do so. As they move up to the number nine position, the same thing can then be applied to the person standing at number seven and the number eight spot. We know that great results bring with them greater rewards.'

'And greater people create greater results?' suggested Billy.

'That's right,' confirmed Alex.

'So, lots of little changes are more effective than one big one?'

'They can be, yes, Billy, and very often absolutely are.' Alex was impressed by Billy's astuteness.

'Once you have a number of people in the team moving up the scale,' Alex expanded the theory, 'filling voids as they go, those next to them then have the choice to move also, to stay in touch with those near them, or remain resistant and stay where they are.'

'What happens to those who choose to remain resistant, Alex?'

'Well, eventually, there is a bigger void that can appear and those people are in danger of alienating themselves from the rest. Instead of the leader alienating themselves, the great leader is able to build the team so that those wanting to hold the team and others back alienate themselves, and then leave themselves the choice to join the rest or realise the team isn't really for them and it's time to move on.'

'That sounds a bit harsh,' challenged Billy.

'It may sound harsh, but have you heard about synergy, where the productivity of a team is greater than the sum of individuals in the team?'

'Yes, we studied that on my course.'

'Well, no one person is greater than the team. Teams by definition have no place for individuals and individuals who want to do their own thing can only do their own thing on their own.'

'So a great leader enables a team to work together to move to where they want to get to collectively?'

'Yes, and this is called the rubber ring principle, when everyone in a team is pulling together to achieve the shared goal or collective objective.'

'What's the rubber ring principle?' asked Billy.

'Imagine one of those large rubber rings you can use as a buoyancy aid in the sea or a swimming pool.'

'Like a tyre inner tube?' clarified Billy.

'That's the kind of thing. Now imagine there are a number of ropes attached to the ring, say eight, and there are eight people standing around the rubber ring. Each person then picks up one end of a rope and walks away from the ring until the rope is almost taut. If, collectively, they all pull out gently at the same time, the ring will lift and levitate in between them all.'

'I can imagine that, yes,' confirmed Billy.

'Good. Now, if one person in isolation decided to pull hard on their rope because they wanted to move the ring in their direction, what would happen?' asked Alex.

'The ring would distort and be pulled slightly in that direction,' guessed Billy.

'Yes, probably, and what do you think the others would do?'

'Pull back themselves to maintain the equilibrium?'

'Quite probably, yes. Now imagine that the first person to pull loosened their grip and the ring reverted to the original position and shape. This, in turn, triggered another person to pull in another direction, in their direction. What would happen then, Billy?'

'The same thing in another direction, I would think.'

'Correct,' said Alex. 'Different people pulling and pushing in their own way, doing their own thing, expending energy and effort but without direction, so the ring stays in the same place, just potentially damaged and distorted.'

Billy reflected for a while.

'So the ring is the team or club and the members are those holding the ropes?'

'You've got it, Billy. So if the team want to move the position of the ring, what is required?'

'They all need to work together, know where the ring has to end up and then they can work together to manoeuvre the ring accordingly,' suggested Billy.

'Exactly and great leaders encourage the team to establish their current position, get buy-in to agree the desired outcome or goal position for the ring, make sure everyone in the team knows what's expected and then empowers the individual members and the team to work out what they must all do individually and collectively to achieve the desired outcome. Great teams have great individuals do great things together, with collectively understood direction. In my experience,' Alex continued, 'This principle also extends beyond the members to the leaders. Most clubs, societies, organisations have regular changeover of leadership, many defaulting to one-year terms with changeovers happening at annual meetings or AGMs. This leads to something I refer to as "one-year-isms". This is where from one year to the next successive leaders – chairs, presidents, masters – pull the ring in one direction, only to find the next leader pulls in another direction, and so on. The end result being, years down the line, the rubber ring is pulled and stretched but hasn't actually moved. The organisation is in the same place despite the hard work and effort of all the preceding leaders. Great leaders, however, stop the rot. They respect the fact that the club is bigger and more important than they are and they set in place a structure that will develop the organisation through others.' Alex concluded, and the two sat in silence for a moment or two.

Alex was reflecting on the experiences he had observed and been a part of that supported this view of great organisations over failing ones. Billy sat, looking at the passion for success in Alex's eyes. It was inspiring that someone cared more about the success of others and the success of great organisations ahead of their own success. Billy was amazed. The two finished their coffees.

'Next week, Billy, I'm meeting with a group of friends of mine. We're going gliding at the local aerodrome. I'd like it if you came along as my guest.'

'I'd love to!' Billy exuded his usual enthusiasm in his acceptance. He felt honoured to be invited and they made arrangements.

There are some wonderfully great benefits of changing leadership on an annual basis: it brings a natural refresh to the role; it avoids stagnation; it allows for a sense of succession; and it does not burden those members volunteering to get involved with too much load to carry. However, there are also a lot of negative side effects of regularly enforced changes of personnel and it is these that I refer to as "one-year-isms".

We have previously looked at the need for long-term goal setting – beyond one year. Short-term one-year-ism planning leads to inconsistency, pulling one way and then another, that just confuses the general membership or an organisation and leads to a lack of trust and confidence in the leadership. In these circumstances, members will avoid reacting to changes or new ideas simply because, from experience, next year or the year after that things will be done the old way again.

A lot of organisations find themselves stagnating when faced with such neutralising of efforts and this in itself can make for a more difficult journey out of that place, even when the membership in general knows something needs to change.

One organisation I have worked with used to pride itself on changing all leadership roles annually – to refresh its members and to be vibrant, fresh and dynamic. The challenge was that one-year-isms were bringing the organisation to a faltering dead stop. There was no long-term vision. There was neither a plan nor a sense of direction, and the organisation was imploding with many of the volunteers ploughing lots of hard work, time and money into their hobby to find no reward, no thanks and no impact at the end of it all.

A long-term plan was agreed upon:

• A single person was given the responsibility to oversee the implementation of the plan.

- All volunteers worked on the delivery of the plan.
- Successive leaders understood that they were not more important than the organisation.
- Volunteers took on longer term appointments to create some stability and consistency.

The club has since found a way to move the metaphorical rubber ring collectively in a single direction, while keeping it levitated, moving it to a place from where greater successes will emerge.

What great clubs, societies and organisations have in common are great people attending a great programme of events and turning up with great attitudes, so that everyone leaves feeling better for attendance rather than drained. Some of the best organisations have specific teams working on future meetings and events that are fun, entertaining and provide something a little more than expected, so the members and their guests feel like they are getting something better than anticipated.

Golf clubs or societies enlist the services of a good speaker to liven up the awards ceremonies. Some clubs even pay for their captain, while they are still in the role of vice-captain, to undergo professional speaker training so as to avoid boring and mundane post-match dinners.

More 'service' clubs are adding value to their members with training, fun events and relaxed agendas to remove the stuffiness that can be associated with their meetings.

Even organisations steeped in hundreds of years of traditions, etiquette and protocol, such as some of London's City Livery Companies and Guilds, have in recent years put on specific events designed to attract and be of interest to younger members and prospective members – to become the members of the future.

KEY LEARNINGS

All organisations do well to remember that each member that brings a guest along as a prospective member does so by putting their reputation on the line. It is well known that the best recruitment channel for organisations is their current membership. So, if an organisation has a declining membership they need to look at ways to regain the trust of their membership to put their name to its name. They will only recommend the organisation if they can be assured their reputation will be built up and not destroyed. Therefore, the organisation has to live up to and exceed expectations. This might be at a local, regional, national or international level and obviously preferably at all levels. Every organisation is judged through each and every member and each and every member is the organisation.

In order to achieve greatness this has to work both bottom-up and top-down. Those at the top must lead by example, lead with greatness, take control of their attitude, exude enthusiasm for the organisation and live up to the expectations of the public about what the organisation stands for. They must walk the talk. Leadership in most organisations today is not the job of the chair, president, general secretary or master, it is the role of *all* those involved at a high level, no matter what their job or role – vice chair, warden, court assistant, secretary, treasurer, to list only a few. They should all hold in mind and act 'presidentially' or 'masterly'.

The recruitment of new members is not the sole remit of the membership officer or the membership committee, but every member of every committee. Without members the organisation ceases to exist, the need for volunteers ceases to exist and those who feel themselves as too important to put membership ahead of themselves will cease to have importance.

Each and every role should assess all that they do, everything within their remit and in their part of the plan and ask 'How will this improve membership?'

I worked with one guy, a treasurer at the time, who had to present the 'boring numbers stuff – the stuff that makes everyone fall asleep'. With some coaching and guidance, he was able to present his message beautifully in tune with the plan in a way the membership understood, bought into and were inspired to implement. He got results others hadn't. He walked the talk of membership being at the heart of all that he did.

Great attitudes of individuals make for great meetings, no matter what is on the agenda. Great meetings mean a great programme, no matter what is planned or arranged. Great programmes mean members will have the confidence to invite guests knowing their reputation is safe. Great organisations have prospective members wanting to become members because they can see the added-value that being a member brings over not being a member.

Some clubs have a policy of 'leave your work at the door'. Some have a fine system as a fun way to instil great ways to behave. Some have changed their programme to reflect what the membership would recognise as great and some have instilled a curfew on meetings so the boring bit is done early in the evening – sometimes before a meal – allowing more social time. Whatever you do to achieve this is not important so long as, individually and as a group, you do what you need to do to create the environment where greatness can show up and reside.

How do great organisations attract great people? The answer is two-fold: they do actually attract people who would otherwise not be great, and they are the making of the greatness in that individual. Great organisations know that members are what make the organisation great. Great members know they are only mere custodians of the membership and will pass on tomorrow to others who will benefit from the greatness they instil today.

Chapter Nine
Flying and Playing Rugby

Chapter Nine Flying and Playing Rugby

Billy lived in a modest maisonette which he shared with two other guys also on graduate schemes for other employers in the town. Billy's flatmates' rent was paid for by their respective companies, but Billy paid his own rent from his hard-earned, modest income. He, therefore, had the 'box room', which was the smallest of the three bedrooms and commanded the slightly lower rent.

The flat was located above a shop in the centre of the quiet mainly residential town. There were about 70 or so similar flats and maisonettes above shops and offices, predominantly occupied by either young professionals working in the area or retired folk wanting to be within walking distance of all the amenities.

Billy's abode was one of six two-storey maisonettes in a row above a block of six shops, in a side road off the main high street. Access was gained via steps at the rear of the property, guarded by a rusty handrail and railings, which saw the occupiers and their visitors on to a large, flat roof extending along the whole block making the shops more spacious than you'd think. All six maisonettes had a front door that opened on to the flat roof. Some had pots of flowers outside, others temporary washing lines. It was like living in a little terrace one floor up. To Billy, it was home. His career had begun, this was the first step on the ladder and he was intent on enjoying the journey rather than just waiting for the destination.

Billy's flatmates worked in offices and so headed home to their parents most weekends. With Billy working in retail, he worked every weekend and rarely headed home. He enjoyed the weekends because, with his flatmates away, he had the run of the place. He chose what he liked on the TV and made himself 'at home'.

During the week, when his flatmates were there, Billy spent a lot of his time reading business books in his room, listening to audio books on his headphones or cooking batches of food – he had learned that this was the most economical way to feed yourself.

On this particular Tuesday night, Billy was alone in the flat while his flatmates were at the pub enjoying a post-work 'cold one'. It was a gloriously sunny evening and the day had been a scorcher. The doorbell rang at two minutes after six o'clock. Billy had been through the personal checklist he had in his head at least half a dozen times, yet, when the doorbell rang, he still felt unprepared.

Alex had told Billy to expect Stuart to pick him up at six o'clock. He'd suggested that Billy wore loose-fitting comfortable clothing and had advised him he'd be wearing denim jeans, a rugby-style shirt, trainers and a lightweight jacket in case of any rain or a chill in the air as the evening wore on.

'Sorry I'm a bit late,' Stuart said, as Billy opened his front door. 'You must be Billy?'

'Yes.'

Before Billy could ask, Stuart continued, 'I'm Stuart. Pleased to meet you. I've heard a bit about you from Alex and you sound like a great chap. Have you ever been gliding before?'

'No, I haven't.' Billy patted his pockets to check he'd got his keys and his cash and picked up his jacket that hung on the wall behind the open front door at the bottom of the stairs. 'Have you?' he asked, not really concentrating as he went through the checklist in his head one more time, patting his pockets and pointing at his clothes as he went through the list.

'Have you got everything?' Stuart ignored the question to ensure Billy was fully prepared to set off.

'Yes, thanks.'

'Good. Shall we head off then?' Stuart stepped out of the front door and let Billy lock up.

He waited for Billy to turn to him and smile a more relaxed smile, 'Yep, ready to go,' confirmed Billy.

'To answer your earlier question,' began Stuart, 'Yes, I've been gliding a few times actually; it's an amazing feeling when you're up there. I won't spoil the experience for you. I'll let you enjoy it for yourself and we can talk about it on the way home.'

'Do you live around here, then?'

'Fairly close.' Stuart went on to describe to Billy where he lived and Billy reckoned it must have been about five miles out of Stuart's way to come and collect him.

'It's kind of you to agree to collect me and bring me back too.'

'No problem, we do this for all our guests. One of our members who lives close will be asked to play driver. It just makes everyone's first night more relaxing and enjoyable. It also means you can have a drink if you'd like,' replied Stuart.

'So, how many members do you have?' enquired Billy.

'Around 24 now. We used to have fewer, but we made a few changes to how we operate and how we go about what we do and we have attracted more and more members.'

'Will they all be there when we arrive?' asked Billy, nervously apprehensive of walking into a large group of people he didn't know and feeling lost amongst a crowd.

'Most will be, but they'll not be there when we get there. We should be one of the first there, which will mean you'll get the best flight I reckon,' Stuart said, looking up to the sky through his windscreen.

Billy could hardly believe that Stuart seemed to know instinctively what he was thinking, what his apprehensions were and relaxed him by assuring him without any effort.

The rest of the journey was spent talking mainly about Billy, what he was doing, where and what he'd studied, how he'd ended up working in Alex's firm, what interests he had outside of work and all manner of things so that Billy felt himself relaxing, not like he was being interviewed.

They pulled up on the make-shift car park next to a port-a-cabin on the airfield. Stuart led the way into the flying club's clubhouse. As they entered, Stuart took the lead. 'Hi. We're here for the group trial flights tonight,' he said to the man behind the reception desk.

'Oh, yes. Good evening gents. Two of your colleagues have already arrived and are through there in our lounge area,' he pointed at a double doorway into another room. 'Once there are enough of you, we'll take you through to one of the briefing rooms for the first briefing and get you airborne.'

'Sounds excellent,' said Stuart, as he led the way into the lounge.

Billy was wearing a slightly nervous smile and felt very excited about his first ever trip in an aircraft. As they entered the lounge, Billy recognised one of the two members – it was Alex.

'You'll know Alex, obviously,' Stuart gestured towards Alex.

Alex immediately stopped what he was working on, came across to them and the second man followed suit.

'Evening, Billy,' welcomed Alex. 'Good journey?'

'Yes, thanks.'

'And this is Neil, our chair,' Stuart introduced the other man.

'Hi, Billy. Pleased you could make it this evening. It's a great evening for flying. I'm sure you'll really enjoy yourself.'

Stuart handed Billy a can of cold drink, 'We'll save the harder stuff until after we've been flying,' he said.

More small talk ensued and before too long more members had begun arriving. As planned, the first group of trial pilots were whisked off into a briefing room and after about a 20-minute briefing that covered safety drills and how any aircraft stays in the air, the first two delegates were invited to step forward.

Billy was not in the first brace to head skyward, he stayed with the others in the first group and, one by one, Stuart introduced them all to him. Billy spent a few minutes with each one making further small talk.

Billy was feeling very relaxed when the chief pilot appeared at the door, 'Next pair to go then.'

Billy was ushered forward by the other delegates and spent the next half an hour in the sky. The time literally flew by. The pilot gave him instruction throughout, advised him what they were doing, what they could see and even let him take the controls for a while.

After a comfortable landing, Billy headed back to the clubhouse, where more members had arrived and others were partaking in another briefing session. Billy could feel the adrenalin circulating through his body and he knew he was wearing a huge smile. He really did enjoy the experience as much as everyone had led him to believe he would.

Stuart bought him a drink from the bar and, before long, Billy was meeting other members a few at a time. They all seemed very pleasant and friendly and everyone was making Billy feel very welcome. Neil and Alex also joined him for a chat at one stage and they talked about flying and the experience. Billy described the eerie silence in the cockpit of a glider and the sensation of looking down over the towns and villages below.

Before long the barbequed food was ready to be served and, again, Billy was pushed towards the front of the queue. Alex and Neil had prepared the barbeque and the two of them were now serving the food. Stuart made sure that Billy always had a drink and was never left alone, nor was he overwhelmed by a madding crowd.

As the evening went on, Billy relaxed more both with the company and with the effect of a couple of beers. 'So, Stuart, you mentioned on the way here that you made a few changes in how you operate. May I ask what changes?'

'Sure. We removed our dependence on doing things the old-fashioned way. We modernised.' Stuart answered.

'How did you do that?' enquired Billy.

'Well, first we all agreed that we had to change because we were losing members and not replacing them. Someone once said "If you carry on doing what you've always done, you'll always get the same results." If we had carried on burying our heads in the sand, we'd have lost all our members and would have been forced to close the club.'

'Wow, that sounds quite serious,' commented Billy.

'It was. So we talked about possible ways forward. Then we agreed that talking wasn't going to change anything. The talking had to stop and the action had to begin. We all had to put aside any differences as to how we achieve our goals and agree on one single way forward, and then all play our part in doing what we needed to do to get ourselves there.'

Billy's mind drifted back to the rubber ring principle; here it was being demonstrated in action.

'Once we agreed to all adopt the plan and play our part, we could work on devising the plan. We needed to create a club that guests wanted to be part of and members felt proud to invite people to, so the structure had to be right.'

'So what did you do?' Billy encouraged Stuart to keep talking.

'We agreed who the next five chairs were going to be and who was going to adopt the year-long role for the next five years. That gave us the stability and the time with which to build. Previously, we had drifted in different directions one year to the next as different chairs did their own thing and inflicted their own ideas on others. In fact, I was one of them yet I didn't realise until we went through this process of change.'

'That must have been a bit embarrassing,' suggested Billy.

'Not at all,' continued Stuart. 'On the contrary, it was enlightening to realise I was part of the problem and that I, too, had to change to ensure I was going to be part of the solution and not remain part of the problem.'

The two went on to discuss how the club wanted to maintain its traditions, but also had to attract new members who didn't particularly care for some of those traditions. Rituals, toasts and recitations that were felt to be inappropriate were dropped from proceedings. Chains of office ceased to be worn. Jackets and ties were replaced with 'modern business dress' so open-necked shirts and jackets became an option.

'Once we had our future secure for more than the next 12 months, we could begin to plan accordingly,' said Stuart. 'The next thing to put in place then was our programme of meetings and events.'

Stuart went on to describe how the club had drifted into boring mundane meetings, arranged at the last minute by the chair without much forethought, planning or consideration.

'So how did you overcome that?' asked Billy.

'It was Norman's idea really. He was the first of the five chairs I mentioned. He included all of us in choosing our programme, something we'd never done before. We used to leave it up to the chair to decide and, of course, not everyone likes the same things as any one individual.'

Stuart went on to describe how Norman had turned up to a meeting with a pack of sticky-backed note pads and a bunch of pens. He asked the members attending to first write down all the events (one event per note) that they had attended previously and had really enjoyed and wanted to do again. As the notes were being written, Norman collected them up and displayed them on one wall, bringing together those ideas that were common. Next, Norman asked everyone to write down the events they had done that were awful and should never be repeated. Again, these were displayed, this time on another wall. Lastly, he asked for everyone's ideas of things they'd always wanted to do, but had not done yet.

'That sounds excellent,' said Billy. 'So, then you chose the ideas that had the greatest contributions?'

'Not quite,' interjected Stuart. 'That's what I had begun to think, but Norman took things a stage further, which was just masterful.'

Stuart went on to describe how Norman had then created a list of the ideas. The club first were surprised how many events they had been doing year in year out that a number of members felt were bad and should not be repeated. They agreed to drop them with immediate effect. Norman then asked each member to score their top 15 ideas for each category – old meeting ideas and new meeting ideas. Once scored, each member had contributed to the meetings and events that Norman then included in his programme – those which had received the highest scores.

'It meant more members turned up to more events because they had chosen them and been a part of the process to select the programme. Norman had great support throughout his year.'

'Why was the scoring system so important?' asked Billy.

'Well, it became apparent that some meetings had been suggested by a number of us, one idea in particular springs to mind. However, once we were asked to score it that idea scored poorly, despite it being suggested by more than half the members,' explained Stuart.

'I see.'

'Likewise, there was one suggestion that was only mentioned by one member but that got the highest score. You see, just because only one person had thought of it didn't make it a poor idea.'

'That's fascinating,' commented Billy, and instantly began to think about how he could use the idea to help his team at work decide the right way forward and all be included in the process.

'The other great thing that came from the exercise was that there were so many great ideas shared that not all of them could be allocated into one year's programme. So Norman's work influenced the programmes for the next three years. We have recently repeated the exercise and have got more great ideas coming forward particularly from the new members,' enthused Stuart.

'It sounds like you made quite a few radical and fundamental changes. How did the members take to the changes?' asked Billy.

'There was plenty of apprehension and concern, but we all knew something had to happen otherwise the club would cease to exist. The key, I think, was that everyone was involved in the process of decision making in the first instance and we all agreed to play our part in moving our rubber ring to a new place. Sorry, do you know about the rubber ring principle?'

'Yes, Alex has told me about it.'

'I think the other factor is what I call the Rugby factor,' Stuart continued.

'What's that?' asked Billy.

'I used to play a bit of rugby in my youth. Have you ever played?' Billy nodded. 'Well, I used to play lock forward or second row and I used to jump to catch the ball from the line-outs.' Billy nodded again. Stuart stood 6ft 5in tall and possessed such a broad set of shoulders that his physique left Billy in no doubt of his suitability to play rugby and play in that position too. 'A few years ago,' Stuart continued, 'They changed the rules to allow other players to lift their fellow players in the air at line-outs. You often now see players catch a ball that is 14 feet or more above pitch level. Back in my day, we would be lucky to get a few inches off the ground. The rule was changed for a very good reason.'

Billy had begun to wonder where on earth this was all going.

'Imagine if you didn't agree with the rule change. The referees now play to those rules and other teams do too. Whether you like it or not, the rules have changed. That decision is out of your control. What is in your control, however, is how you react to the changes.'

'How do you mean?' quizzed Billy.

'Well, if you stuck your heels in the mud over the rule change and agreed with your team mates that the old way was the best way, and that things should not change, and you all agreed to not lift your fellow players in the line-outs, how many line-outs do you think you would win during a match?'

'Not many, I'd say,' laughed Billy.

'Precisely. I'd say probably none at all. And that might put you at a huge disadvantage and may even jeopardise your chances of ever winning a match.'

'So, sometimes, if rules change, you just have to accept them and get on with playing to the new rules?' asked Billy.

'Exactly. Especially rules that are outside of your control or you have no influence over. You see, we realised that society had changed, members' lives had changed and potential members' lives had changed too. They wanted something different. The differences they wanted though were not completely opposed to what we already had on offer. They didn't want circles turned into squares…'

'They wanted circles turned into spheres?' Billy felt good being able to contribute to the metaphor.

'Yes. Alex has shared a lot with you, then?' Stuart asked rhetorically. 'So we have modified what we do and how we operate and the increased number of members we have and the overall increase in atmosphere we now experience at our meetings makes it all worthwhile. I'd say we now all get so much more out of being a member than we ever had previously.'

'With your structure in place, your common goals, your programme and teamwork, what happened next?'

Stuart then went on to explain that by creating the environment where the members began to have a good time, and with regularity in the programme and every meeting being great, a sense of pride returned to the club. That pride led to members feeling proud enough to put their personal reputations on the line by inviting friends, family and colleagues along to meetings. In fact, a number of members introduced acquaintances they had had only very little contact with. There had been many more guests coming along. Not all of them had stayed, some had relocated and others had found work or family circumstances meant that they had had to change their priorities, but it was accepted by the membership that these things happen in life.

Stuart went on to say that the good name of the club in the town had been improved since they also looked at every opportunity to demonstrate the club existed, that its members have a great time and that they are open to new members joining.

'We found there were lots of people who would have joined much sooner, but they didn't even know we existed, where we met or really what we did. Some knew about us but we realised that they wanted to be asked to join. They would not come forward voluntarily as we had previously thought.'

'How did you let people know about you?' asked Billy.

Stuart went on to explain that they operate as a non-profit club. There are no vast amounts of money for marketing and the like, so they set about identifying opportunities to tell the public about the club. They looked to support other local clubs and societies with manpower and, in exchange, they were able to secure contact with members of the public, some of whom may be interested in becoming a member and some of whom knew someone who might be. They made a note of which houses made a donation to their annual appeals and sent them a 'Thank you' card with an explanation of what they do, inviting them to make contact or find out more. They began to offer the first meeting for free, so another barrier to a guest's first meeting was removed. Lastly, they began to make regular contact with the local press and, slowly but surely, they began to see the club being mentioned more and more in the local papers. The events and activities they ran received publicity. One of the members produced some posters and these were placed around the town.

'It's about identifying what you do that can be used to your advantage and maximised to let the public know all about you,' explained Stuart. 'We were amazed how little extra effort and time was required to make the most of what we already did.'

As they were leaving, Alex came over to check Billy had had a great night. He apologised for being engaged most of the evening looking after the members with food and beer. Billy commented at how well Stuart had looked after him and the two arranged to meet at Archie's Place the following week.

The journey home seemed much faster than the journey to the meeting. They talked about Billy's first flying experience and Stuart gave

Billy a copy of their forthcoming programme for him to have a look at to see if he'd like to attend more meetings.

Billy lay in bed reading the programme imagining himself one day being a member – maybe even being chair, running the sticky-note exercise that Norman had done a few years earlier. He'd had a great night.

One club that used the sticky-note exercise after hearing me speak at an event had superb success with not only making sure their own members had excellent attendance, but they would even regularly attract members from neighbouring clubs to their events. It was even known for a member from another club to bring a guest along to their meeting.

Another club used to suffer the fate of many other clubs with business meetings descending into long-drawn out affairs arguing over where to donate cash or how to raise the cash. In one particular year, it was agreed by all members to outline a three-year project to raise funds for a specific cause. This relieved the ongoing debates and arguments. It meant meetings were better attended and it meant there was a more amiable atmosphere into which the members began to invite guests.

I have also known a club line up a number of chairs in advance for several reasons, but the main reason always appears to be the same... stability. For instance, a club that has three annual chairs lined up has a future history of at least three years. A club with only this year's chair (and there are some that don't even have a vice chair) has a future history that runs out in a few months' time. Prospective members and guests will quickly get a sense of this and ask themselves: 'Who would want to be a member of a club that may close in few months' time?'

Making your guests feel special is paramount. This does not mean going over the top, but certainly arranging to collect them and return them for their first meeting is a very simple way to include them and make them feel welcome.

There are some clubs that pass members from a younger version to an older version – for instance, Cubs to Scouts, or Scouts to Venture Scouts, Rotaract to Rotary, Leos to Lions, Round Table to 41 Club, etc. What is important for the 'older' club to recognise is that when a member leaves the younger club it can still be as daunting as their very first meeting. There may be members whom they don't know; there may be rituals or protocols they are unaware of. It is like leaving primary school and heading up to high school – daunting.

Imagine if Scouts who moved up last year, and therefore probably know Cubs who are due to move up this year, were encouraged to 'buddy' their known previous fellow members for the first meeting or so. Imagine the positive impact of a Rotary member picking up a Rotaract graduate member on their first couple of Rotary meetings. There can be an induced sense of unease and feeling like one of the 'inbetweenies' and it can make even adults feel like being back at school, despite having a number of years of experience under their belt.

Clubs like this that encourage older members to be involved with the younger club and enable younger members to have a 'taste' of the older club will encourage greater uptake and transition. Those who consider the transferring member to be a new member without any knowledge or understanding will, in my opinion, engender a sense of welcome, care and warmth where others will not.

I know of one club – and more since I have been sharing the idea – who used to collect money for local charities at Christmas with Father Christmas on a sleigh towed behind a vehicle around the residential roads of their town in December. One year, they decided this was an ideal recruitment opportunity. Their driver, who had previously sat warm and bored driving at 5mph all night, was given a job. He was given a clipboard, a pen and sheets of paper with the road names at the top of each. Being the driver, he knew all of the roads. All he had to do was capture the numbers of the houses of possible recruits. Collectors would engage the householder for the usual couple of minutes and simply shout the number of the house to the driver, who'd capture the number. After all the routes had been completed, the club had a list of contacts. They sent postcards to all of those houses thanking them for their donation and told them how the funds had been used from previous years. They also invited the householder to get in touch to attend a forthcoming meeting. From this, the club attracted an extra six members in just one year.

I was asked to attend one club's 'new members' night – like an open night if you will. There were a number of prospective members there and during my address I asked them to consider what event or activity they had always wanted to do and, if this particular club offered it to them, if they would join tomorrow. I then asked them for their ideas: we got wine tasting, tank driving, bird of prey flying, tractor driving and abseiling, to name a few. With all the ideas elicited, I then turned to the chair to ask if any of those items were on their programme during the next two years. The chair gave the perfect answer: 'They are now!' How many of those prospective members actually became members do you think?

In the modern day, clubs that engage with social media well are the ones attracting new, younger members. Clubs that usually attract older members need to take note because the younger members of today (by this I mean up to 45 years old) will soon be in the age bracket of these older clubs and they will not have a way of engaging with you in the way they have become used to engaging with others. The new technology has to be embraced... like it or not – it's a rugby ruling change you just have to accept and work with if you are to survive.

It's interesting to note that there is an inter-livery group for younger members of London Livery Companies. These organisations are 400–500 years old, and they are embracing social media as one of the ways to communicate with their members and prospective members.

KEY LEARNINGS

Think about the events you run or are involved with at the moment and think about how they may be used as a recruitment platform:

- Do you run a Santa collection? See above for ways to utilise this to your advantage.
- Do you run a major community event? I have seen it before where the club is so busy running the event that they have no hands free to run a membership stand. So enlist the help of other clubs – either your neighbouring club, your older or younger club, if you have one, or other service club that may offer you manpower for the event to allow two or three of your members to run a membership stand.
- Run a raffle with people answering a couple of questions that may help you to assess their suitability for membership. Gather their contact details and bingo you have a database. Bear in mind there are strict rules governing the use and security of databases these days. Make sure you comply with the rules and you will be ready to go. This method is very simple with probably only a case of beer, wine or an experience day being your financial outlay.
- Help run community events to ask the public to join the organ donor register, blood donor register, etc. and use the time to engage the public with your club.
- Find out what events are run by other clubs and offer to help. When your club needs help, the other clubs will be more willing to help so you can have extra manpower for your own membership stand.
- Work with your local press to increase your profile in the papers and always include contact details.
- Make sure you have a good website that is current and fresh.
- Engage with social media.

Chapter Ten
The Elephant Story

Chapter Ten The Elephant Story

'It was as the door closed that it began.'

Alex had been telling Billy about a childhood experience he'd had. He'd been brought up in a holiday hotel, which meant that as a family there were never any traditional family summer holidays because work, income and guests came first. Holidays were, therefore, restricted to winter time and often weekends away to London. Alternatively, during the October half term, the family would dash up to Blackpool and catch the 'last weekend of the lights' – the famous Blackpool Illuminations.

As the holiday industry began to enjoy some fabulous years where the town was often full to capacity with every hotel bed filled, business became good for the family. They began to enjoy foreign travel and Alex and his brother were lucky to be able to enjoy some great holidays.

*****

One particular year, while his older sibling was living away at university, Alex and his parents had been bound for Sri Lanka, formerly known as Ceylon. Alex had been just 12 years old. He had learned to appreciate his growing-up years and he considered himself to be extremely lucky.

At the time, his father had been a member of a local service club for some years and had become chair the year of the trip to Sri Lanka. The organisation was an international one and so, being proud of his position in the club, he had written a letter to the chair of a club in Sri Lanka. This was back in the late seventies, the days before the internet, mobile phones, facsimile and globalisation. In fact, even international phone calls were unheard of because of the vast expense involved. The family received no reply to the letter.

The flight had been a lengthy one and, in those days, families were not well catered for on air travel. Air travel was only just becoming accessible to the general public having previously been the reserve of the upper classes, businessmen and women and the military. Hotel accommodation had only begun to appear in recent years and facilities were generally basic. However, the expense and the surroundings were worth it to get to enjoy some 'guaranteed' sun.

When they had arrived at Colombo Airport in Sri Lanka it had not been a patch on the departure airport of Heathrow, which had been one of the most modern airports at the time. Nevertheless, the warm welcome they received had made up for that.

It had been 6 o'clock in the morning and the outside temperature was already soaring. Alex recalled how the heat had filled his nostrils and the sound of chirping locusts had filled his ears as he stepped off the aircraft, with the heat shimmer visible above the runway as its temperature rose. He had been shattered from the long journey, but excited to be in foreign lands.

'It was more of a large tin shack, than the modern, brick-built property that we have come to expect today,' said Alex, as he described the arrivals lounge to Billy, who was listening intently to the story absorbed by every word.

Alex then went on to describe how haphazard the facilities of the airport had been. Baggage collection had not been a fancy carousel; suitcases had simply been unloaded off the aircraft and left in lines on the tarmac for the passengers to collect themselves. Passport control had been conducted by a team of three officials sitting behind trestle tables, and customs had been managed by a bunch of scary military personnel brandishing guns and stern faces.

The airport had been quiet, as though this was the only aircraft to have arrived so far that day. There had been a sense that the airport operated on a one aircraft at a time basis. The only passengers in the large hangar had been those from Alex's flight who were ushered towards a large open area where representatives from a few companies stood with placards.

Between Customs and the Holiday Representatives had stood an obviously local man, alone, holding a placard with Alex's family name on it. Alex's father had told Alex and his mother to stand where they were and watch over their bags while he approached the lone man. As he had approached the man, one of the representatives had also approached the man and Alex's father.

After a short discussion, the checking of documents and some good-natured gesturing, Alex's father had returned and said, 'Okay, come and follow me.' And the family had followed the man with the placard out of the building and into the car park. Their luggage was loaded by the man, who had refused help from Alex and his father, and the family had clambered into the car.

In the car, Alex's father had explained to his mother that the man knew of their arrival, had all of their details, knew which hotel they were staying in and had been sent to collect them and take them to the hotel directly, thus avoiding the need to be transported on a bus with the other guests. Alex's family had checked into the hotel, unpacked, eaten lunch and had been relaxing in the afternoon sun cooled by a perfect onshore breeze sipping iced tea by the time the rest of the British holidaymakers had arrived by bus. Those also arriving from Heathrow had been hot and bothered, having waited in a non-air-conditioned bus for over two hours for a second plane to arrive from Manchester.

The evening had been spent exploring the hotel facilities and enjoying the balmy climate, while sipping local cocktails expertly produced by the barman, Jackman, who had introduced the family to his speciality non-alcoholic cocktail that became Alex's favourite drink of the holiday – the 'Jackman Special'.

The following morning, the family had awoken with all the eagerness and excitement one wakes with on holiday, refreshed by a good night's sleep under mosquito nets and ceiling fans in the colonial-style hotel. Off they set for breakfast, served in the hotel restaurant which opened out on to the poolside veranda. As they had passed reception, the same man who had driven them from the airport sprung up from his seat with a beaming smile.

'Good morning, sir,' he had smiled. 'Where you want to go today?'

Alex's father had explained that they just wanted to spend the day relaxing by the pool, exploring the vicinity to get over their long flight.

'Okay, sir. I'm here for you, sir.' The driver had sat himself back down, still smiling.

The next day the same thing happened on the way to breakfast. Then the next day and the next one too... It had quickly become an expected norm. After about a week, Alex's father finally went to chat to the local man after breakfast, partly out of curiosity, partly out of guilt and partly out of embarrassment.

During the week, Alex had made friends with two boys of a similar age from a family that had also flown out from Heathrow. (It would be later established that they lived only a few minutes' drive from Heathrow and Alex and his family would pay them a visit on their return to the UK to freshen up after the long flight before their long five-hour drive home.) The three amigos had played all day in the pool and in the grounds. They had watched wildlife, played table tennis, snooker, draughts and a myriad of local games, though they had no idea what they were called. They had learned the rules from the local staff who had enjoyed the willingness of the boys to embrace the locals and their culture.

That afternoon, Alex had emerged from the pool for lunch to overhear his parents discussing the driver. It turned out that this fellow was one of the house staff of the chair of the local club to whom his father had written weeks before. He had sent his driver and a car to collect them from the airport knowing it would ease the final part of their journey. He had also sent him to the hotel every day with a car to take the family wherever they wished to go.

Messages had then been subsequently passed backwards and forwards and, over the next few days, the two chairs had met. It had become apparent to Alex's father that it would be rude to not avail themselves of the gesture, and so they had planned a trip to the central mountainous region of the island to visit Kandy in the heart of the tea plantation countryside. The local chair had arranged everything with infinite detail. They were to have a private tour of a plantation given by the owner, an acquaintance of the chair, followed by lunch in the residence resided in by Lord Louis Mountbatten whilst visiting Ceylon, run by a business associate of the chair.

The day started early and the hotel had made special arrangements with the staff to open the restaurant early to provide the family with breakfast. As one might expect, the driver had been at the hotel waiting before the family had even appeared for breakfast. Soon after breakfast, they were off. The Mercedes saloon with plastic-coated seats would have given a very comfortable ride had it not been for the numerous pot-holes in the roads. There had been no air-conditioning back then and it wasn't long before the sun came up and the windows had to be opened to ease the stifling heat. Alex recalled how his hair had thickened with the red dust that filled the air.

On the way, it became apparent that the driver spoke very good English and the source of his language education had been his love of cricket and, in particular, English cricket. He would listen to the commentary of BBC World Service radio transmissions for hours. He knew the names of all the players, something Alex didn't know that well having spent all his sporting hours playing and studying rugby.

Alex had been fascinated with the wood and corrugated iron-clad shack-style buildings lining the roads, the Singer billboards everywhere – a name that was synonymous with sewing machines and cars in Sri Lanka – and the abundance of Singer cars and sewing machines around. Alex also recalled the roads being red. Well, more of a pink than a red. The tarmac used for the roads had obviously been of a lower grade and cheaper material than that which Alex was accustomed to. Along the sides of the roads had been huge piles of broken sea shells every couple of hundred metres or so, inverted cone-shaped piles standing eight feet high. It was established that the shells were used to hold the red tarmac together in times when the sun heated the material to the point when it changed from a solid to a liquid and the tarmac began to escape its desired position and slip into the verges. (Alex would later go on to share the story with many people, beginning to doubt his apparition of red roads. Finally, one day someone at a seminar confirmed they, too, remembered the presence of red roads in Sri Lanka. So Alex knew it was true and that his memory served him well.)

'Mr Sir?' the driver had asked Alex's father, who was sitting in the front passenger seat.

'Yes.'

'Would you like drink, sir?'

There had not been much hesitation from the three passengers; Alex's stomach had begun to think his throat had been cut.

With a 'Yes, please' vote cast, the driver had pulled the car off the road and on to the verge alongside a solitary hut literally miles from anywhere. The driver had leapt from the front seat and begun a conversation with the owner of the hut. The owner had jumped up quickly and grabbed a machete that was lying on an upturned wooden box. He'd been sitting on a second box that was stood long ways on its end. In his other hand, he adeptly manoeuvred a large, green fruit twice the size of a melon turning it with precision in the very tips of his fingers. With each sweep of the machete slices from around the top fell to the ground, as he masterfully shaped the upper third of the fruit. He expertly lopped off the top with a perfectly delivered horizontal blow. The flesh of the top third of the fruit was exposed but had not been punctured. He then struck the top four times with vertical downward blows. On the fifth blow, he pierced the fruit with the point of the machete. He removed the machete with a flourish with an almost perfect one-inch cube of the flesh attached to its tip. With the same movement he lay the machete down on the makeshift table, picked up a transparent plastic drinking straw, slid it into the hole left by the removed cube and handed the coconut to Alex with a smile and a nod of the head. Alex had felt like applauding but he had his hands full. He had watched with amazement as the hut owner performed the same clever display two further times with just as much precision. The second coconut was handed to Alex's mother, the third to his father. The taste was out of this world, not just because of the parched condition of Alex's throat, but the sheer freshness of the milk of the fruit. Each fruit housed a good quantity of liquid and it took some time to drink it, all of which the family savoured.

Just as they had been finishing their drinks the driver appeared on the other side of the road. Alex had not even noticed that he had disappeared, having been captivated by the machete skills of the hut owner.

'Mr Sir, Mr Sir,' he had called from across the road, peering out from the foliage of the bush and beckoning the family to cross to where he stood. 'I have surprise for you, follow me.'

Alex's parents had looked at each other with one of those looks of apprehension and concern that parents are able to give that asks all the questions that can be asked without uttering a single word. Alex had waited for one of them to make a move. His dad had nodded to him and Alex had dutifully followed the driver, taking care to step in exactly the same place as the driver did, placing his front foot as the driver lifted his back foot. They quickly emerged from the tall grasses at the top of a river bank, looking down the bank to where loggers were working with elephants in the river and on the banks to pick up and move the colossal logs with ease, loading them on to waiting boats to transport them up river.

'You want to take picture?' the driver had asked, miming out taking a photograph and then pointing at the camera around Alex's neck.

'Sure,' Alex had said, starting to remove the camera from around his neck.

'Not here,' the driver had said. 'Down there.' He had pointed down the bank towards the elephants and, again, led the way with an encouraging, 'Come, come.'

They had followed him. Alex removed his camera and took photos.

'On his back,' the driver had suggested. 'These are my friends.' He had then pointed to the workmen. 'They are happy for you to get on the elephant's back for picture. They are quite tame.'

Everyone had looked at Alex. Two images had been running through his mind. The first (and better image) had depicted the elephant throwing him off and trampling him into the river. The second had been an image of the elephant rearing up and running off into the bush with Alex holding on to its ears gripping on for dear life, followed by a long line of little Sri Lankan men with their sticks running behind powerless to stop and capture the beast with Alex on its back dashing into the bush never to be seen again. He would never see his family again.

'Erm, no, thank you,' Alex had said, as politely as he could so as not to cause offence.

Alex's mother had been offered and she had clambered on to the elephant's back and had posed for a photo. As she had slowly got down from the elephant, Alex had been offered a second time.

'Erm, no, thank you, really.' He had taken longer to answer this time. He watched as his father climbed on to the elephant, posed and had his photo taken before dismounting. Alex had quizzed his parents about what it had felt like. They had described the short, stubby hairs tickling and scratching the bare flesh of their legs clad only in shorts and the vista from so high over the grasses across the planes beyond the river. They had both worn massive smiles. Alex had been offered a third time.

*****

'It was only as the door closed that it began,' Alex said to Billy, who was as captivated by the story as Alex had been with the hut owner, 'It being the regret,' Alex continued. 'The regret that I never did get on the back of that elephant. You know, I carried that regret with me for a very long time. Every time I faced a challenge and I questioned myself. There was this little voice inside my head reminding me about the elephant, reminding me that I had a history of just bottling it, reminding me I had a history of not having what it takes.'

Billy sat in silence just looking into Alex's eyes as he drifted into a world where he was obviously recounting the times he'd talked himself out of success.

'You see, I can recount the story to you today like it was yesterday, Billy,' Alex continued. 'I've played it over and over in my head time and time again like a movie in my mind, with all the detail like it happened only yesterday. You see, I know what it is like to have regret. Regret that holds you back, regret that stops you achieving. Whatever you do, Billy, never allow yourself to regret anything life passes your way. Grasp every opportunity with both hands. Face up to your fears and live to celebrate your decisions, not to regret them.'

'Sometimes it's good to not do things though, isn't it?' questioned Billy.

'Sure, like picking a fight with a crocodile or waking a poisonous snake,' replied Alex. 'You see, great leaders are able to assess the situation, grasp the opportunities and stick to the decisions they make. There is a lovely saying I heard from someone I once mentored: "It's not about making the right decision, it's about making the decision right!"' Alex quoted.

The elephant story is a personal one – like many in the book – and is often the one that moves me the most. At home, I still have the photograph of my mum on the back of that elephant. I now have positive thoughts when I think about that elephant.

So, how can a story that is not only personal but also based on an individual's experience have any relevance to a club, a society or any group of any kind?

I strongly believe it does.

As an individual, we may ask questions of ourselves or make negative statements about ourselves:

- Remember when you last failed?
- You failed this last time.
- You won't achieve that goal.
- You're too young.
- Are you not too old to be attempting that?
- Remember that elephant?

It is no wonder that the world of sport is fully embracing the use of 'sports psychologists' these days. At a less professional and far less competitive level, the art of controlling 'internal communication' is just as important if we want to achieve the successes we desire.

By 'internal communication' I don't just mean at an individual level, although this is very true and your members may well be asking or saying the following:

- What will I gain by joining?
- What's in it for me?
- Can I be bothered to attend tonight?

- Will I get to sit next to 'x' or 'y' – they bore/drain/energise/entertain me?
- I'm too young to do that job/role.
- I'm on my way out and can't be bothered anymore.
- In my day it was/wasn't like this.
- We'll never manage that.

By 'internal communication' I also mean the communication within a club at a local level:

- We don't have enough members.
- Our programme's boring.
- Not another dinner/dance/charity event.
- We should attend this – but I can't go.
- We'll never beat them.
- Oh, we are rubbish at that.
- Our members wouldn't be interested in that.
- We all like to sit in our own little clique of friends.

Also, at higher levels, such as regional, divisional or national, we have to be wary of 'internal communication' that portrays a sense of the following:

- You should do it like this.
- You should not do that.
- Another month of falling membership numbers.
- We are having a great time up here spending your money.
- Look at me, aren't I important?
- I want to do things my way.

So, if any of the above examples ring any bells with you, your club or organisation, or you can imagine them or similar things happening, then the organisation has an internal communication voice that needs to be modified. Things need to become more positive so that the members at large are proud to be associated with what the organisation stands for.

There is very little difference between organisational 'self-talk' that holds a club back and individual 'self-talk' that stops us achieving our goals, or indeed stops us getting on the back of an elephant.

It is entirely sensible, however, to not plough ahead regardless of any real dangers which may lie ahead. For instance, just because someone on TV approaches deadly snakes and handles them, does not mean any one of us can do it. Do not jump off the cliff just because others tell you it is safe.

- What kind of internal organisational self-talk are you aware of in your organisation?
- What are the real dangerous things you should not attempt under any circumstances?
- Which moments do we just need to seize?

KEY LEARNINGS

One of my strongest learnings over time has been the inability we seem to have to act on 'negatives'. What I mean by this is, we often act on the implied positive rather than the negative. Confused? Good! From confusion normally comes clarity, so let me explain...

In a seminar situation, I will often ask the audience to close their eyes. I paint a picture of relaxation – maybe sitting on a beach with a glass in one hand, book in the other, perhaps listening to favourite tunes. Then, in that place, I command the audience to not visualise a big, pink elephant in a tutu dancing in the sea. And I even repeat that under no circumstances should they see a big, pink elephant dancing in a tutu in the sea.

Try it on your unsuspecting friends and/or family. Watch their faces smile as they are unable to avoid seeing the elephant, even though you have told them not to.

So when giving instructions or asking members to do things, it is important to state your desired outcome in a positive style rather than as an expression of what you do not want.

Now that you understand this principle, imagine the sports team that is ahead with minutes to play and the call goes out: 'Don't give away any penalties'; or 'Let's not give the lead away'. Can you imagine what all the players are now thinking about? Can you guess what may well happen in the last few minutes? So what might they say instead? How about: 'Stay onside', 'Keep it clean' or 'Let's stay ahead'.

In membership organisations, you may hear things like:

* Don't let our members leave.
* This is going to be a failure.
* We always rely on a willing small number..

How about replacing these with:

- How can we retain our members?
- What do we need to do to make this a success?
- Let's encourage all members to be involved.

A common concern for clubs with dwindling numbers is the difficulty in having enough members to take on the organisation of an event to raise the club's community profile. Any event will cost greatly in terms of members' time and/or effort. This is where clubs need to think and work smarter and possibly work in partnership with other clubs. Partners can be sourced within the same organisation from neighbouring towns or cities, or from other organisations or clubs within the town.

I recall hearing about a small town that had the largest membership nationwide in a number of different organisations. Thus proving that community belonging encourages more community belonging and as one club grew so did the others. Working together can have a far-reaching impact.

One organisation could organise a firework display, for instance, and be helped by another. In return, the second organisation could run a carnival and be helped by the first.

If neighbouring clubs work together, one could organise an event while the second could help by manning a membership stall, for instance. Or rather than holding, let's say, three low-attended events organised by three different clubs, imagine one massive event attended by all three clubs and all their respective guests, all having a better, cheaper, more positive event... with, likely, more guests invited and maybe more members as a result.

What are the negative language patterns you have heard inside your organisation? What are the ways we can replace negative language patterns with positive ones?

Chapter Eleven

Horns and Haloes

Chapter Eleven Horns and Haloes

'Someone once told me,' Alex continued, 'That you only regret the things in life that you don't do, not the things that you do.'

Billy now sat very thoughtfully, wondering what his 'elephant' was. He had certainly imagined a number of things about himself over the years: I'm not bright enough; I'm not good enough; I'm stupid; I'm useless; I'm not old enough.

'Snap out of it,' smiled Alex, who'd stopped talking a while ago and had been sitting watching Billy internalising things. Billy jumped and smiled when he saw Alex grinning at him. 'Penny for 'em?' Alex asked.

'I was just thinking about all the times I've had negative thoughts that have held me back or stopped me doing things – my elephants,' Billy said.

'It's good that you recognise them,' went on Alex. 'The next steps are to accept they are not the most resourceful things to be thinking about. Consider what you might more positively say to yourself in a similar situation in the future, put them behind you, learn from your mistakes and move on. Otherwise you'll also do what I did and carry the regret around with you for years and years, decades, in fact.'

'Wow, really?'

'Yes. It took me quite a while to slay the demon that was my elephant, but, you know, it stopped holding me back well before the story ended.'

'How did the story end then?' pressed Billy.

'I'll tell you that later,' said Alex, knowing that Billy was back in a resourceful place, a place where he was ready to learn again. 'First, you need to know how to seize the opportunities that will present themselves to you.'

'Okay.'

'Remember the mentor I mentioned before?'

'Yes,' answered Billy, back to being his enthusiastic and eager self.

'Well, he used to have a simple saying that really helped me to focus my mind on the task in hand and it has made me take action sooner rather than later. He used to say to me "Get in first boy", and I never knew the real significance until much later in life.'

'Another hidden gem like building a jigsaw?' asked Billy.

'Precisely,' responded Alex, knowing the young man had learned so much already. 'Back then, it was about the importance of getting to a customer or client before they got to you.'

'How do you mean?' asked Billy, with a confused face.

'Have you ever placed an order for something and found its delivery was delayed?' asked Alex, safe in the knowledge that for most people what follows confusion is clarity and learning.

'Yes, and rather frustrating it is too.'

'So what did you do?' asked Alex.

'I picked up the phone to ask them about the order. They took my details and said they'd call me back in an hour. They didn't. I had to call them back for an update.'

'What was the updated position?' asked Alex.

'That the product was found to be faulty and had been rejected. They had specially ordered a new product for me and it was being shipped the next day.'

'So they pulled out all the stops for you then?'

'Yes,' answered Billy, 'but, I was still upset.'

'Why was that?' enquired Alex.

'Because I had had to call them back. They had promised they would call me back within the hour but they didn't. I wasn't sure until the product arrived whether they were not just fobbing me off!'

'You see,' continued Alex, 'it is more important to communicate with the customer than getting the situation resolved. Don't get me wrong, both are important, but if at the point where it was identified there was a fault, and before you called the first time, they had called you to explain the situation and their actions, how would you have felt then?'

'I'd have still been upset, but the fact that they contacted me as soon as a fault was identified, I'd have thought how diligent they were, that they cared about my order and were not just processing the order like any other job. I would have been very pleased that they had taken appropriate action and treated my order with priority.'

'And if the product had arrived a day later in each instance, how would you have felt?' probed Alex.

'In the first instance, like I had been fobbed off and lied to and would probably have thought about not using them again, and, in the second instance, I'd have been more patient, thinking they were obviously checking the product carefully before sending it out.'

'You see, you'd have been more patient if they'd got in first than if they had ignored the situation.'

'Definitely,' concluded Billy.

'This is something I call the horns and haloes effect,' said Alex.

Billy had a quizzical look on his face, a look Alex had become familiar with.

Alex went on to explain that people form opinions very quickly and often will base their opinions on the views of others, instead of forming their own. He went on to describe how in the modern world we are bombarded with the views and thoughts of so many others through TV, radio and the internet, as well as discussions, and all too often gossip or untruths are presented as facts. He went on to explain how the mind works: 'It is only capable of assimilating a small number of pieces of information at any one time, despite being bombarded with images through the eyes, sounds through the ears, smells in the air, sensations on the skin and such like, making up millions of pieces of information at a time, things you hadn't even been aware of until I mentioned them.'

Billy instinctively scratched his head, not because he was thinking but because until that moment he had not been aware he needed to scratch.

Alex went on to describe that, in order to cope, the mind filters the information and this has been studied by many experts in the field. He explained to Billy that in order to cope with the amount of information in the world it is easier for a lot of people to simply accept the word and view of others, rather than to establish the facts for themselves and form their own opinions. 'Imagine, if you will, a retailer that you think offers poor service. Now, if you visited them and you got poor service, what would you think?'

'That it was to be expected,' answered Billy.

'Exactly,' said Alex. 'They have only confirmed and strengthened your viewpoint or opinion. Now imagine visiting them and receiving great service. What would you think then?'

'That it's a one-off, a fluke or maybe a new member of staff,' suggested Billy.

'Exactly, you make excuses for your opinion. You look for reasons why the experience was not right and your opinion is correct. Now think of a retailer that you believe offers great service. Now imagine going there and receiving great service. What do you think?'

'That they have just confirmed my opinion again,' replied Billy, confidently.

'Yes. Now consider going there and getting poor service. What do you think?' asked Alex.

'That it is a one-off, that it is normally good so it must be due to a new member of staff or just a bad day.'

'Precisely. You see, you make excuses for your opinion and the experience. It is so important to wear a halo in the eyes of the client rather than horns. Whichever you wear, it is hard to shake off the image clients have – to change their opinion.'

Alex then went on to say that sometimes people form those opinions based on the views of others. They also might group an organisation together with others they view as being similar and, in these instances, any association needs to be broken to demonstrate the disassociation.'

'How do you mean?' asked Billy.

'Do you know the story of *The Ugly Duckling?*'

'Yes.'

'Well, there you are. Because the baby looked and acted like an ugly duckling, it did not allow itself to portray the image of what it really was, which was a beautiful gracious swan,' explained Alex.

'Oh,' blurted out Billy, who was having a flash of inspiration. 'That first club I went to, they all wore ties and suits, and there was another group who didn't.'

'So when you sat having a drink and observing, what did you think of the two groups?'

'One was old fashioned, stuffy, exclusive and elitist. The other was young, modern, trendy, fun and exciting.'

'I see, and you formed that opinion based on what exactly?' Alex posed one of his wonderfully timed rhetorical questions, then after a short pause continued. 'And which one did you think you'd rather be associated with?'

'The second group.'

'How long did it take you to form that opinion?'

'A very short time indeed really.'

Alex went on to explain that the information he had been made aware of had led him to believe that the time most people take to form an opinion about others is about seven seconds only. Billy was amazed, but at the same time could relate to that. Alex then went on to ask if Billy knew from what point the seven seconds began to be measured. Billy had no idea, so Alex again explained that it was his understanding that this was from the point that someone is aware of another's existence.

'You see, Billy, you formed those opinions sitting in a bar, without them knowing you, without them knowing you were there, without you even getting to know them.' Billy started to feel a bit guilty. 'But don't concern yourself, Billy,' Alex added. 'Everyone does exactly the same.'

Alex continued the lesson and made it clear to Billy that the purpose was to understand that we form split-second opinions about others and they do about us. Great leaders know this to be true and by being themselves and being true to who and what they are others can form the best opinion of them. They also know the importance of slowing down their own opinion-forming mechanism, so that they can form factual opinions based on the truths they see and get to know the other person first, and not rely on gossip or folklore.

Alex also explained about the part of the brain called the reticular activating system that controls our motivation. It controls what we are/ are not attracted to. It's the part that lets us see what we want to see through all those millions of pieces of information the mind is assimilating all the time; it allows through what we want to filter. So, if we want to see 'stuffy, old-fashioned' behaviour to support our views of what jackets and ties represent, then that is what we see. If we want to see 'open-neck shirts and laughter' as young, modern and exciting, then that's what we see and how we interpret those experiences.

Therefore, it is critical that an organisation portrays the right image that will attract the people they want as members towards them. If an organisation wants to attract tie-wearing, etiquette-upholding, traditionalists to join them, then they should dress like them. Likewise, if they want to attract young, great, fun-loving individuals, then they must dress, act, behave and be like them.

'People like people like themselves,' concluded Alex. 'Great leaders know this and know the importance of being yourself in order to attract people like yourself towards you. They are able to get the best out of others by understanding their motivations – something we'll look at later. They know how to maximise any opportunity that presents itself to them. They understand not to take people at face value and the need to get to know the real person underneath. They know how quickly people form opinions about them. They truly know the value of word of mouth marketing, the power of recommendation and the power of talking the same language to their team, members and clients.'

Alex concluded their meeting for the day. 'This is what *carpe diem* means, Billy. Seizing the moment of an opportunity to avoid living with the regret for a long time to come.'

I have a good friend from whom I have learned a lot about public relations. He runs courses and acts for a number of very high-profile clients. He regularly reminds me, as anyone in that industry would, that it takes a lifetime to build a great reputation and can take only a second or two to destroy it.

Some modern-day examples of this include Gerald Ratner and his infamous quote about the quality of his company's product for the prices they sell at. In the wake of the Deepwater Horizon oil spill, BP's name and reputation has been significantly impacted, especially in America. Companies and names like this have to work much harder to regain their reputation than companies who work to maintain a reputation that has not undergone a significant negative event.

I know of a lot of trainers who during their work make comparisons to sports personalities when emphasising the need to practise, practise and practise. The point being made is that it takes many repetitions to hone the skills to be truly great. Trainers will talk about sportsmen and women practising their skills even when they have reached the top of their field. Many used to use Tiger Woods as an example before all the media hype surrounding his alleged indiscretion. Almost overnight, trainers across the globe stopped using Woods as an example and began talking about Roger Federer.

The public's expectations also change over time. I remember the time when Marks & Spencer was the name other retailers wanted to be compared to for service. Very soon after, it was John Lewis. Currently, I believe the retailer that the public use as a benchmark is Apple. Their service is incredible and soon not only will that level of service be the stand-out benchmark, it will become the norm, the expected norm and, eventually, even that level will no longer be good enough.

In the same way that all retailers are currently compared to Apple, all clubs and societies will be compared to those levels of experience. The public expect to be treated, cared for and looked after in those ways. Clubs that think they are not compared to experiences their members and prospective members receive from other sectors of society are on a very slippery slope.

With reference to clubs, societies and organisations, some conjure an instant image rightly or wrongly in most people's minds, which is often based on either someone else's opinion or an experience they may have had with a similar organisation, especially if they know nothing about the organisation.

There was one person from whom I learned a lot about recruiting. I learned that he did not mention the name of the club he was a member of when inviting a prospective member along. For instance, he would simply ask, 'What are you doing next Tuesday?' and with the answer 'Nothing' he would proceed to invite them to join him with a bunch of friends to a night out, doing this activity or that, having a beer or a meal. Once there, the individual would meet the others, get to know them, experience the atmosphere and the greatness of the meeting and, invariably, at some point ask, 'So how do you all know each other?' and it would be at this point only that they would talk about the club.

When I asked my friend why he felt this worked, he explained to me that if you lead with the name of the club, there is a risk that the individual will already have an image as to what the club is like, what they do, etc., or will compare it incorrectly to other clubs. He found there to be inherent misconceptions or prejudices towards clubs and societies that people didn't know about already. He found that by using this approach he was able to circumnavigate any of these and replace them with the reality of the great club he was a member of.

People like people like themselves. So imagine, for instance, if a shy, retiring type of character is 'buddied up' with a loud, extrovert character. It may not be the best match for a first exposure to a club. In my experience, great leaders are able to find a member with a similar character to buddy a guest, which makes for a more enjoyable experience for all and is more likely to progress to membership sign up.

However, what all clubs need to be very aware of these days is the fact that it is easy for non-members, customers or clients to find out all about you before you are even aware of them. Between an invitation being sent out and a guest attending a meeting, be aware that it is most likely that they will have visited your website, searched you on the internet and possibly read any other material there is on you out there in the ether. So, not only is it good practice to ensure you have a website, it is essential that it is up to date and current.

KEY LEARNINGS

Well, some of you may be thinking, that's all well and good and makes sense but how do we do that? In order to seize the opportunities of converting guests or prospective members to be paid, signed-up members of your rank and file, there are a few pointers to bear in mind:

- Ask them – it is amazing how many times I have heard people say they are waiting to be invited to join, yet members are waiting for the individual to ask to join. This lack of communication needs addressing. There are some clubs who do this well, they do it early on in the process and they are expanding.
- Have a chat with them – more and more clubs hold an informal discussion with individuals before asking them to be members. This is not an interview (although some organisations may well retain this style of selection); it is an opportunity for the individual to ask any questions they may have and for the club to set out their expectations of members so that no embarrassing misunderstandings are revealed later. This can be done by telephone or, with the use of modern technology, via the internet. It can also be employed not just at entry level but is often successfully used when selecting volunteers from within the organisation too.
- Buddy – some of the most successful clubs have a buddy system. This not only gives the individual a 'hand to hold' or a 'friendly ear', it also acts as a conduit to help them understand proceedings. For instance, if mnemonics, internal jokes or abbreviations are used, the buddy can explain these so the individual can quickly settle into their role feeling like they belong. It helps to dispel any assumed levels of knowledge.
- People like people like themselves – ensure their buddy or at least the people they sit with are of a similar character. Your club may even have great communicators who are able to universally communicate well with just about all characters – use them in this role.

- Process – even if there is not a formal process, ensure there is at least some sort of agreed process. This helps the members to understand the process and the individual to know where they fit in. Make sure the process is neither too long nor too short, and make sure it is used to ensure fairness for all guests and members.
- Make it special – when you do induct a new member, make it special for them. Some clubs have specific induction processes, speeches or rituals. Ensure it is memorable; we'd all like to think we can remember our investiture. Make sure the individual knows what to expect – no one likes surprises. Make sure they are welcomed by all, receive a welcome pack that explains things to them and gives them contact information and, if appropriate, ensure they receive a team uniform so they feel part of the team from the off.

Chapter Twelve

Black Ties and Bungee Jumps

Chapter Twelve Black Ties and Bungee Jumps

As Billy approached the café, he could see it was bustling and busy. There was a real buzz about the place, more so than normal. The sun was shining bright and the air was warm. Billy guessed that Archie must be working today. The place was only ever like this when Archie was on duty. Billy thought back and smiled to himself as he reminded himself he was having a great day and who was responsible for that.

The café was packed, there was not a table free anywhere, except one solitary table – it was Billy's table.

Alex arrived only a moment after Billy and Archie delivered their usual order to the table without them even needing to order.

'On the house today, sirs.'

'Why's that?' enquired Alex.

'I've had a number of parties visit the café this week, sir, all asking if I was Archie and saying that I had been recommended by your friend Billy, sir. It's my way of saying thank you.'

Billy sat smiling, very proud that so many people had taken up his recommendation and that it had been appreciated.

'People only recommend places they know their reputation is safe with,' Archie turned his attention to Billy, 'So thank you for your trust and confidence, sir.'

As Archie left the table, Alex said, 'You've made an impression there. Thank you, too, for making sure that my reputation remains intact.' Alex knew that his reputation was strengthened and weakened by those he was known to be associated with and especially those he was known to be mentoring.

'So, what are we going to cover today?' asked Billy.

'Well, our journey is drawing to a close, Billy. We have looked at backward planning, the seven mistakes, building jigsaws, and doing sums. You have experienced greatness and heard Archie's story, and know that great teams understand the rubber ring principle. You have seen the importance of identifying opportunities and how great teams are brought together by great programmes. Last week I shared with you my elephant story, the need to get in first, horns and haloes and that great leaders seize their opportunities because they understand the meaning of *carpe diem*. All we have left is the last element, Billy.'

'Nurture?' asked Billy.

'That's it,' replied Alex. 'Nurture. Now, although it's last, I'd say it is possibly the most important element. I say this because all the other elements need to be in place before this one can be most effective.'

'Like the last pieces of a jigsaw?' asked Billy.

'Similar, yes,' Alex continued. 'But, remember, not all of the pieces will be put in place during this process.'

Alex went on to tell young Billy that great leaders understand the 'Gardener's Rule' – that the work you do today bears fruit next year. He told Billy that great leaders are able to prioritise their workload efficiently, making sure they spend their time wisely on the important things, and at a time that allows them to do it well. Whereas many managers and unsuccessful leaders spend a lot of their time working on important tasks but at the last minute, which often means they are inefficient, mistakes occur from the rushed completion and, as a result, more work is created. They know about effective delegation and the associated empowerment, and they know what needs to be done and what is simply a distraction.

'Before I first joined my club…,' started Alex.

'The club that went gliding?' Billy interrupted.

'Yes. I went to visit a number of others clubs first. I've always been one of life's belongers. I was always in one club or another – the local rugby team, Cubs and Scouts, university basketball – until I started work. After that I had no social life, no friends outside of work. I was lost. So I thought about joining a club of some sort. I'd heard good things about some clubs and some not so good things about others, so I decided to try a few first.'

Alex went on to tell how he had also been along to the club he first introduced Billy to, run by John and Peter. He told him about his first meeting. The meeting was given a special name, but it meant nothing to Alex at the time. He was told to turn up at the same restaurant that Billy had attended. He'd made contact by telephone, arranged times and places by phone but had not met anyone previously. He turned up wearing a suit and tie, not knowing what to expect. He'd thought if I'm overdressed, I can always take my tie off.

Alex told how he had turned up as Billy had done and there were two groups at the bar, as there had been on Billy's visit. He had sat and had a drink. When he had finished his drink, he approached the barman to ask about the club he'd arranged to meet.

'You're a bit underdressed for that lot,' the barman had said, as he gestured towards the group wearing dinner jackets and bow ties.

'Do they always dress like that?' Alex had asked the barman.

'No, just a couple of times a year.'

Alex went on to say how embarrassed and excluded he had felt standing there. He had asked the barman to not mention the conversation and had turned on his heels – he had been too embarrassed to even let them know. Alex had then sent them a cheque in the post the next day with a short note making his apologies, never to return.

The next week, Alex had rolled up at the same restaurant and approached the other group of men. He had approached one man and told him about his story and that they looked like a great bunch of guys to socialise with. They had bought him a drink and had made him feel very welcome.

'It's quite funny, really,' one of the men had said. 'Over the years I've been coming here, our numbers have grown while theirs have reduced.'

'So how do you all know each other?' Alex had asked.

'We've all had the same experience, and share only that. It's the same experience you've had – turning up to meet a club only to find that you just don't feel like you'd fit in, and then approaching this other club at the other end of the bar. I don't think the other club knows who we are or how we all met.'

Alex told Billy that one of those men introduced him personally to a friend of theirs who was involved in a club. The man had made sure that both men came along to one of their social drinking gatherings and were introduced. They seemed to have a lot in common and Alex had felt very comfortable accepting the invitation to attend the club, of which he was still a member. Alex had been given a lift to his first meeting, just as Billy had. Like Billy, Alex had enjoyed his time and he was made to feel extremely welcome, just as Billy had been.

'You see, Billy, first impressions really do count. Someone once said "You don't get a second chance to make a first impression" and it is so true.'

Alex went on to explain that whilst being a member, he had never stopped learning; he'd never stopped picking up new ideas or concepts. He had completed a number of roles within the club and the club ran on a 'team' structure, so that each role was undertaken by a team with a team leader, someone who had done the role before and someone who was new to the role. That way, the club preserved the knowledge it had built up. It also meant that roles were not onerous because the easy way to achieve results was passed from team leader to team leader.

All the roles were well defined with expectations set as to how success would be measured and then, once agreed, individuals were left to achieve the success with occasional reporting back to the overall leader.

'Great leaders know how to delegate, empower and then trust their team to deliver,' said Alex. 'They know that clear direction and agreed goals are the roots to a successful delegation. They know that when giving direction it should be done in private, yet praise should be given publicly.'

Alex went on to tell a story of a friend of his who had been asked to do some coaching and mentoring with some managers and supervisors for a local company. After an initial group session, the team had been split into small groups with each group being set some tasks to perform during the interim weeks. When they had got back together, they had been asked to share their experiences.

One man from one of the groups had told a personal story of how he thought the initial session had been a waste of time; he felt it was all nonsense and after a couple of weeks decided to challenge his learning.

He had played for a six-a-side football team. They had been bottom of the league – they had not won a match in years, nor had they scored a single goal that season. They would always blame each other, shout at each other and be over-critical of each other's play. It had not been a nice team to play for. Then he had remembered one night on his way to the sports hall about one of the things talked about in one of the group sessions – the power of encouraging. 'What did they have to lose?' he had wondered. There were only two matches left in the season. So, he committed himself to only giving positive praise during the match. He'd shout 'Good effort' instead of the usual 'Why didn't you pass?'; 'Next time you'll score' instead of 'That was rubbish'; 'Right idea' instead of 'What did you do that for?' The end result was that they scored four goals. They still lost 5–4 in the last minute, but they had really celebrated that night.

He'd observed that his team mates had copied his encouraging style too, with others shouting encouragement instead of abuse to each other. Although they lost, they had certainly all had a much more enjoyable evening of social sport. The following week they won the last match of the season. Alex quoted his friend's mentoree: 'You'd have thought we'd won the FA Cup'.

'Lastly,' said Alex, 'Great leaders know that different things motivate different members of their team. Do you play golf?'

'No, I never have,' answered Billy.

'So, if I asked you to perform a task for me and said that if you performed it really well, then I'd buy you a round of golf at a famous golf course, or a new golf club, or even offered to buy you a set of clubs and a new bag, how motivated would you be?'

'Erm… not very,' admitted Billy.

'Precisely. So tell me what do you like?' asked Alex.

'I like things like bungee jumping, abseiling and parachuting. I've never done any of them, but they all look great.'

'Perfect. So would you rather a £50 round of golf or a £50 bungee jump?' offered Alex.

'The bungee jump.'

'Okay. What about a £500 set of golf clubs or a £50 bungee jump?' suggested Alex.

'The bungee jump again,' confirmed Billy.

'Why?'

'Because I've always wanted to do one. I don't care too much for golf,' said Billy, honestly.

'It's interesting, isn't it, that you'd take something much less expensive financially because the personal value to you is greater?'

'Yes,' agreed Billy.

'Great leaders know the value of personalised motives and that people are not simply motivated by hard cash amounts.'

Billy was smiling at his ability to again understand something that so many other managers and leaders had told him was the most difficult part of their job.

Alex continued, 'Great leaders know how to create the environment for their team where they feel empowered but also safe to make a mistake, so long as they learn by it, of course. After all, you have to fall off the bike to be able to learn to ride it properly, and you need to learn how to ride first before being able to ride with no hands. Having said that, there is also the need for trainees to trust their mentors and to know when to listen and not get ahead of themselves. Trying to run before they can walk or ride with no hands before they can ride at all may end in total disaster. This is something too many young graduates fail to understand; they turn their back on their mentor, thinking they know best, and only set themselves up for a much greater fall later. A wise man once said: "An intelligent person learns from their mistakes and a wise person learns from the mistakes of others".'

'Great leaders are able to nurture the best out of people, giving them the confidence to do the best they can,' Alex further explained. 'They make them feel part of the team. No matter how great or small their role may be, they realise that everyone playing a role is important to the team and the success of the team. Great leaders know that no individual is greater than a team, not even themselves. They know their future success is dependent on those who they nurture and how they nurture them. They know the real value of succession planning for the ongoing success of their organisation.'

'Great leaders also know the massive resource that clubs of all sorts offer individuals in their teams,' Alex went on. 'They offer opportunities to practise many skills taught or trained in the workplace in a safe and secure environment. They offer the opportunities to individuals to learn from others within the club, to learn sometimes by those others' mistakes. Great leaders realise that members of their team whose welfare is catered for have an outlet that allows them to function much more productively whilst at work. Above all else, great leaders know the value of free learning, especially when that is learning whilst playing.'

Alex went on to explain to Billy that one of the strongest traits great leaders have is the ability not just to train/coach/mentor/teach someone, but the ability to teach how to teach, coach how to coach, mentor on how to mentor, train how to train, because, in this, the future is secured and future successes are assured.

'Now that we have come to the end of our journey, young Billy, it is time for you to start putting your lessons into action. To assist you, I'd like to ask you to do me the honour of joining our club. I know you will benefit hugely and I know the club will benefit too from having you as a member.'

'Yes, please.' Billy's pride at being asked to be a member, and by Alex, exhibited itself as a huge smile across his face.

Alex knew the value of asking for the order; asking the obvious question too many club members wait to be asked. Too many salesmen don't know when to shut up and ask for the order. Too many leaders don't know the power of great questions and the power of silence. Alex knew all of this, masterfully.

The two finished up their coffees and talked about forthcoming meetings, how Billy was going to implement what he had learned at work, and how excited he was to be spending more time outside of work with Alex and his peers. Billy knew he was going to learn a whole lot more. He was looking forward to meeting Stuart again and getting to know all of the other members more too.

'What about the elephant, Alex?' Billy asked.

'What about it?' Alex asked in reply.

'Well, you said the story hadn't finished. If we are at the end of our journey, how will I find out the rest of the story?'

'How about you buy me coffee again next week, Billy, and I'll tell you?'

Clubs, societies, associations, teams, groups and churches will all do well to remember one thing and one thing alone from this book. It is probably the most important part of the cycle and it requires the other elements to be in place. Likewise, the rest can be in place but they would be worthless without the final element. This one thing is best encapsulated in the slogan, 'Nurture never stops'.

A number of personal friends of mine, and others who have heard me speak at conferences, workshops and the like, have shared with me their experience of not being told how to dress suitably for a meeting: some overdressed in a tuxedo for a casual social night; others underdressed in casual attire when everyone else was in their finery. Either way, there is nothing worse than feeling like the odd one out at any event, let alone your first.

Even when a member has been a member for a while – this could be years or, dare I suggest, possibly even decades – if they have not attended a particular event before, we must understand that they neither know what is expected nor what they are doing – they require a degree of nurturing.

Lots of clubs and organisations look to involve their members and encourage them to get involved at different levels, whether it be at club, local, area, divisional, regional, league or even national level. As an individual rises through the various ranks, it can be easy to see why they may cease to move on to the next level and take their experience and knowledge and talent with them. This is often because they feel they are not ready or they are incapable of making the move. Often, all that is required is a little encouragement, a friend to back them up and, most importantly, some nurturing.

It is understood that there are some organisations that offer training to their volunteers. I believe this is a splendid way of saying thank you to the volunteers, but it also rewards them and helps them to do a better job and, let's face it, isn't that what drives most people involved in organisations as a hobby?

I have spoken at charity organisation conferences where they bring together their volunteers for such nurturing. I understand that some international service club organisations provide training to those who commit to stepping up. I underwent training as a cub scout leader when I was a late teenager myself to give me the skills to be a better leader, but also skills I have been been able to use more generally in life.

This all sounds very formal and structured, and it is to a degree, but nurturing in this way is not only great for those directly receiving it, it also filters down through the organisation to the end users, the members themselves. It is this kind of thing that provides some of the greatest value to the members of organisations.

It does not stop there though. At local club level, I have seen new club captains or chairs installed only to be ridiculed, humiliated and made the subject of a metaphoric feeding frenzy of abuse, heckles and pointed laughter. Some call it banter and in some clubs it is expected. However, I warn such clubs against such behaviour.

Imagine, if you will, a club AGM where a new chair is to be installed. There are three new members who have joined since the last AGM, so it is their first experience of an AGM. The outgoing chair introduces the incoming chair formally. The new chair stands to address the meeting for the first time and the heckles begin. I have seen bread rolls thrown; I've seen members deliberately try to distract the new chair; I have even seen an incoming chair encouraged to drink so much during the evening that when the time came for him to address the meeting he couldn't stand.

Now, don't get me wrong, I am not a party pooper. I like a laugh and a drink as much as anyone. However, I do encourage clubs to put themselves in the seats and shoes of those three new members for just a moment and ask them the question: 'On the evidence of what you have just witnessed, how inspired are you to become the chair/captain/

leader of this club?' When I ask this question at conferences, I often get a laugh. This tells me the message has got through. Sometimes we just don't consider the impact of what we take as a bit of fun and a bit of banter on tomorrow's members.

When someone puts their hand up to get involved, they need to be nurtured in that role and, even if they have been a member for many years, they may still need some nurturing. In my experience, organisations that live up to 'Nurture Never Stops' do very well.

KEY LEARNINGS

The Gardener's Rule

Today's seed is next year's plant.
Today's nurture produced next year's fruit.
Today's guest is tomorrow's member.
Today's member is tomorrow's recruiter.
Today's recruiter is tomorrow's committee member.
Today's committee member is tomorrow's team leader.
Today's team leader is tomorrow's club leader.
Today's club leader is tomorrow's regional leader.
Today's regional leader is tomorrow's national board member.
Today's national board member is tomorrow's national leader.
Today's national leader is tomorrow's international leader.
Nurture Never Stops!

Chapter Thirteen

Seeds and Diamonds

Chapter Thirteen Seeds and Diamonds

'Before I tell you the final part of my elephant story, Billy, there is
something else you first need to know,' began Alex.

'In order to receive hidden gems, someone has to be the bearer of
them. Sometimes the bearer is you or me. My father didn't realise he
was sharing pearls of wisdom at that time, in that moment. Neither did
Mr Vincent the maths teacher. Sometimes we share anecdotes, stories,
experiences, and others are touched, inspired and motivated by what
we share. We do not always know, we do not always find out, what to us
appears like a dingy lump of coal, can be a sparkling diamond to someone
else.'

Billy sat listening intently, as ever. He nodded, showing he understood.

'I was very lucky one day Billy,' Alex continued, 'To be invited to
speak at a conference. There were many delegates from all across the
world. During my preparation, I recalled my experience in Sri Lanka, and
decided that I would share my elephant story to illustrate that we should
not make choices out of ignorance, but should make our choices based on
the facts we know to be true, not relying wholly on others' opinions. We
should take control of our own thoughts as informed individuals. I shared
my elephant story with them to illustrate that holding on to regrets may
not be healthy, that not taking opportunities as they presented themselves
may not be fulfilling, yet still sometimes it is ok to sit on the sidelines and
watch, so long as it is from a position of informed choice and not from
a position of ignorance. I also said it was important to stand up to your
personal challenges and overcome them.

'As I completed the keynote and opened the floor to questions my
eye was drawn to a hand that was raised at the back of the room. I invited
the delegate to ask their question. "My name is Adrian, I am from South
Africa, we also have elephants in Africa, and it would be a privilege for
me to host you in South Africa. I will arrange for you to climb aboard an
elephant and put aside your regret, to overcome your personal challenge
forever in my country."

'There was a round of applause, and I made a mental note to talk
with Adrian later. Another hand was raised and I invited the question to
be shared. "Hi, I am from Sri Lanka, I have a family member who owns
working elephants, and I also invite you to return to Sri Lanka, and defeat

your demon where it began." This time there was an even greater round of applause and I felt touched indeed.

'Another hand was raised, "I am Andrew, I am from Germany, We have a large zoo in our country, and I know someone who works with the elephants there. If you are unable to travel to Asia or Africa, please come to Europe, it would be an honour for me to help you banish your demon in Germany."

'It was an amazing conference, I got to speak to all the contributors and I have made many long standing friends from that time. Although I have not been able to visit any of those people yet, their generosity stays with me and humbles me to this day.

'As a result of that conference, I was introduced to, and formed a close friendship with one man, his name is Sakthi, and we stay in contact quite often even now. Sakthi was not at that conference, an associate of his was there and he recounted his experience to Sakthi, and eventually we met.

'He invited me and insisted I visit him in India, and I was pleased to be able to spare both the time and the finances to go and visit him. He looked after me very well, and I was made to feel part of his family. He arranged travel and sightseeing and visits to places where tourists normally don't go.

'Then one day he asked, as we were driving through a small village between city destinations, "You know the elephant story you shared?" "Yes," I replied. "Well I have a special surprise for you now."

'The car came to a stop and we got out, and from the bush came a working elephant with its keeper. Sakthi had specially organised this without my knowledge.

'I got to ride on the elephant, it didn't trample me, it didn't set off into the bush. It was an amazing experience, one that has had greater impact than anyone will ever know.'

Billy sat in awe.

'You see Billy, great leaders know that what you sow, you will reap. Share your knowledge, share your stories, share yourself and others will repay you in ways you cannot even imagine. What to you may be just a silly story, an experience that has held you back over the years, a lump of coal, may in fact be the catalyst that inspires something great in someone else, a sparkling diamond. Sometimes these others may be those you least expect, they may even be people who didn't actually hear you share your story originally.

'From one tiny seed a large tree can grow. From many seeds only a few seedlings will develop, from those few seedlings maybe only one tree will develop. The hundreds that do not develop should not deter you from putting in the effort to grow just one fine specimen, because that one fine specimen will make all the effort worthwhile, the failures will be insignificant, and from that one specimen a whole new stronger generation will emerge.'

After a few moments of silence, the two stood up from the table, shook hands and turned to pay the bill. With the transaction complete, Archie waved them off.

*****

Years passed, and Billy received promotions, continued his studies. He'd remained in employment with BCH and had eventually taken over a store of his own, and was responsible for an area covering four outlets, with teams of managers working with him.

One day, he returned to the café he had frequented weekly in his past and sat down at what he thought of as 'his' chair at 'his' table. He recognised Archie, and Archie recognised him, 'Hello sir, long time no see, what can I get you?'

Billy ordered a coffee, then sat quietly and thought over the years that had passed since he had last sat in this seat.

He was soon joined by another man. 'Hello Joseph,' he said, 'You found it alright then?'

'Yes thank you, Billy?'

Archie placed Billy's coffee in front of him and asked his guest what he'd like to drink.

'So will you tell me about backward planning please?' asked Joseph in an enthusiastic way that demonstrated to Billy that the young man before him had the same level of passion for learning that he himself had had all those years before.

Billy had taken over Alex's job having proven himself in the various roles he'd undertaken within the company and was highly respected as a great leader. Alex had not trained himself out of his job, but had managed to mentor himself into his next job, having found and nurtured the best replacement for himself. He too had been able to take on a number of promotions in the firm as it continued to expand, safe in the knowledge that all would be well in Billy's very capable hands, and he now sat on the company's board of directors.

They both continue to make great leaders.

About the Author

At the age of three, Brad moved to Tenby, Pembrokeshire in South-West Wales where his parents bought their first family holiday guesthouse. Being brought up in Tenby provided an enviable backdrop for Brad's growing up years. The beach was his 'back yard', competitive rugby became part of his life at the age of six, and out of season playing in the streets meant most of his life was spent outdoors.

Sharing his home with guests, and swapping large spacious reception rooms and bedrooms for small temporary accommodation in a room above the kitchen, a caravan in the garden and even the garden shed (and that is another story!) gave him an appreciation that 'customers are king' from an early age.

Brad always loved being around people and being a part of things. At school, he would often sign up to a drama production, a choir competition, and was an active presence in the school charity week activities. He even arranged a charity parachute jump at the age of 17 for children with cancer.

A regularly attending member of Venture Scouts, he also became a Cub Scout Leader, and would also regularly volunteer to help the local Lions club with their fundraising efforts.

After school, Brad headed for London, and qualified in 1989 as a Dispensing Optician, and later qualified as a Contact Lens Optician in 1991. He served his early years at S H Harrold Ltd in Beaconsfield, with his tutor, mentor, coach, friend and cheerleader Richard who introduced him to Round Table and the Worshipful Company of Spectacle Makers.

In 1992 Brad left Beaconsfield for Birmingham and in 1993 opened his first Specsavers practice in Solihull, with his business partner and brother

Spencer. They opened a second practice in 2008 and continue to run both stores today.

Brad has lectured at Anglia Ruskin University in Cambridge, examined for the Worshipful Company of Spectacle Makers and facilitated workshops for Specsavers. Outside of his professional commitments, Brad has also become recognised as a prolific professional speaker and a communications coach, as well as a qualified Toastmaster.

Since 2003, Brad has been involved with Round Table, holding a number of posts including membership and development officer on the national board from 2006 to 2008. In 2012 Brad joined the Membership Team at The Worshipful Company of Spectacle Makers, and 2013 saw him take up a post of Assistant to the Court – the equivalent of a board position in other organisations.

Brad married Tammy in 2009, in a ceremony presided over by her father, a retired vicar, in the same church in Mawnan Smith in Cornwall where Tammy's parents, brother and sister were married. Luke was born in 2012, and the three of them are regular supporters of Worcester Warriors Rugby and love spending their holidays together in both Cornwall and Pembrokeshire.

CPSIA information can be obtained
at www.ICGtesting.com
Printed in the USA
LVHW050022180723
752707LV00029B/879